KRAFTS FOR KIDS

Models

KRAFTS FOR KIDS

Models

Fenella Brown

CHARTWELL
BOOKS, INC.

A QUINTET BOOK

Published by Chartwell Books
A Division of Book Sales, Inc.
114 Northfield Avenue,
Edison, New Jersey 08837

This edition produced for sale in the U.S.A., its
territories and dependencies only.

ISBN 0-7858-0622-9

This book was designed and produced by
Quintet Publishing Limited
6 Blundell Street
London N7 9BH

Creative Director: Richard Dewing
Designer: Ian Hunt
Project Editors: Katie Preston and Kathy Steer
Editor: Lydia Darbyshire
Photographer: Paul Forrester

Typeset in Great Britain by
Central Southern Typesetters, Eastbourne
Manufactured in Singapore by
Bright Arts Pte Ltd
Printed in China by
Leefung-Asco Printers Ltd.

ACKNOWLEDGMENTS

Special thanks to the models: Clio Brown,
Arron Charles, Spencer Dewing, Victoria Dewing,
Claire Harrington, and Scott Harrington.

DEDICATION

To Clio, Jago and Merrilees

PUBLISHER'S NOTE

Children should take great care when completing
these projects. Certain tools and techniques, such as
craft knives and using the oven, can be dangerous
and extreme care must be exercised at all times.
Adults should always supervise while children work
on the projects.

As far as methods and techniques mentioned in this
book are concerned, all statements, information and
advice given here are believed to be true and
accurate. However, the author, copyright holder, and
the publisher cannot accept legal liability for errors
or omissions.

Contents

acrylic paints

paintbrushes

paint palette

pencil
sharpener

eraser

pencils

Introduction

How often do you sit down on a cold, wet day or during school vacations and wonder what to do? This collection of model-making ideas will provide hours of interest and fun, as well as teaching you some new skills. If you do not want to make some of the models for yourself, you could make them as gifts for friends and relatives. Most of the materials you will need are inexpensive, and you will probably find the tools and equipment around the house. Colored clay, both the oven-bake and air-dried kind, is widely available in craft and art stores, and you will find the special light wood needed for some of the projects in craft and modeling stores.

It is a good idea to keep your own "inspirations" box. Collect pieces of colored construction paper, feathers, shells, scraps of fabric, dried flowers and seeds, buttons, and beads – anything, in fact, that you might want to incorporate into one of your designs to personalize it and make it unique to you.

It is also a good idea to keep a scrapbook in which you can stick

illustrations cut out from magazines and newspapers. If you have a sketchpad or notebook, jot down ideas for colors and patterns as they come into your head – before they disappear. Artists always do this. Sometimes, just flicking through your sketchbook or rummaging in your inspirations box will give you an idea for something new to make. Use your scrapbook to inspire yourself to experiment with ideas and to adapt the models that are included in this book to suit your own likes and dislikes. Before you begin, it is a good idea to draw your idea quickly. Your sketch need not be accurate or beautiful, but you will find it helpful to have an idea of the overall shape and color of the model you are going to make as a guide while you work.

Each chapter in the book looks at a type of modeling material. The projects within each chapter are arranged in increasing order of difficulty – the first is the simplest, the last is the most complicated. However, if you want to make the dog pencil box, for example, look at the way it is made and see if you can find ways of making it less complicated – paint on

colored
construction
paper

cutting mat

knitting needle

scissors

rulers

poster paints

the features instead of cutting them from wood. Don't worry if you want to make the salt dough plate but think that it looks too difficult. Try making it with fewer shapes or decorate it with shapes that you can quickly cut out freehand. Then, when it is dry, paint it with bright colors or add some glitter.

Some of the projects involve using templates, and these are given full size at the back of the book. Either photocopy or trace the outlines you need and transfer them to stiff cardboard. Cut out the cardboard and then use it to draw or cut around to make the appropriate shape. To highlight safety some of the photographs are bordered with red warning triangles and the instructions are written in bold underlined text.

SAFETY FIRST

The projects are fun to do, but as you work, keep the following in mind:

- Remember that you must always be very careful with sharp knives and pointed instruments. Ask an adult to help you when you need to cut out shapes with a craft knife.
- Be careful about leaving knives, scissors, and needles lying around when you are working – they could be dangerous to your younger brothers and sisters. Put a piece of cork on the end of your craft knife to protect you from cuts.
- If you have made a model that needs to be baked in the oven,

ask for help. It is no fun being burned, so always use an oven mitt putting things in the oven and taking them out again.
- When you have finished for the day, clear away all the materials you have been using and put everything away, making sure that all your knives, scissors, needles, and materials are kept in a box, safely out of the way.
- At the end of the day, wash your paintbrushes and clean any brushes and containers that have been used for glue or varnish.
- Store any oven-bake and air-dried clay that you have not used in an airtight container so that it is ready for next time.

modeling tools

toothpicks

cookie cutters

balsa wood glue

clear, all-purpose adhesive

craft glue

craft knife

wallpaper paste

blunt knife

oven-bake clay

air-dried clay

TOOLS AND EQUIPMENT

PAINT

For the projects shown in this book, we used poster paints and, occasionally, acrylic paints. Acrylic paints are useful because there is no need to varnish them to make them waterproof. Like poster paints, they are sold in art shops, and because they can be mixed to make almost any color you want, you need only buy red, blue, yellow, black, and white. Add a spot of black to make a color darker. A spot of white will make a color lighter. It is easier to make a light color dark than to make a dark color light.

foil

GLUE

One of the easiest adhesives to use is craft glue, which is widely available and sticks nearly everything. It can be diluted with water to make a varnish. Although it looks milky as you apply it, it dries clear, so do not worry about using generous amounts to make surfaces stick together.

The papier mâché is made with wallpaper paste – granules that are mixed in water. These days, most wallpaper pastes contain chemicals to stop mold forming, so take care when you mix and use the paste. Wash your hands thoroughly when you have finished and mop up any spills.

cardboard

salt dough

If you need to stick a magnet or brooch back in place, you will need to use a strong, all-purpose household adhesive, of the kind used for mending broken china.

VARNISH

Poster paints are not waterproof, and when you have finished decorating a model you may want to protect it with a coat of varnish, which will give a smooth, glossy look to the surface. Art and craft stores sell varnish – remember to wash your brush thoroughly after use. Acrylic paint is waterproof when it is dry, so if you prefer a matte finish you can omit the varnish at the end.

PAINTBRUSHES

As in all arts and crafts it is far easier and more enjoyable to work with the right tools. There is nothing more annoying than trying to paint a fine, neat line with a fat paintbrush or trying to cover a large, flat area with a brush that has only a few hairs in it. To begin with, try to have a very fine

wallpaper paste

Plasticine

spoon

rolling pin

marzipan

chocolate

colored marzipan

candy

food coloring

cloves

chocolate molds

cookies

brush (about size 11), a medium sized one (size 5 or 6), and a large one (size 1 or 2).

MODELING TOOLS

Some craft stores stock sets of modeling tools, like the ones illustrated in this book. You can, however, buy them one by one if you prefer. As with your paintbrushes, it is easier to work well if you have special tools to mark lines and textures rather than trying to use an old, blunt knife. Wooden toothpicks, used matches, and old ice-cream sticks can all be used, and you will find that old ballpoint pen cases are extremely useful. Build up a collection of tools that you like to use, and experiment until you know what you need for each effect you want to achieve.

KNIVES

You must be very careful if you use a knife. Unless you are using balsa wood, you can probably make all the models in this book with a blunt kitchen knife and a pair of scissors. Even so, do take care, because a blunt blade can cause a painful cut if it slips. Always cut away from you, and make

sure you are working on a flat, stable surface. Place your work on a piece of thick cardboard to protect the worktop, or, better still, use one of the special non-slip cutting mats that you can buy in art stores. Make sure there is an adult around to help with any complicated cutting.

OVEN-BAKE CLAY

This is a great modeling material to use because it comes in so many beautiful colors. It is more expensive than some of the other modeling materials, so it is often used for small items, such as jewelry, little ornaments, or even dollhouse accessories. It needs to be softened in your hands before you can work with it, but when you have made your model and it has been baked in the oven, it becomes hard and quite strong. The colors can be mixed together to make new shades, so you will need only a few to begin with. There are several different brands available, so you must always read the manufacturer's instructions for baking times and temperatures.

feathers

thin cord

colored
construction
paper

SALT DOUGH

This is one of the cheapest of all
modeling materials. You can either let
your model dry out over a few days or
you can bake it in the oven at a very
low temperature for an hour or two.
When you are mixing the
dough, you must remember to
use all-purpose flour. Self-
rising flour will make your
models rise like cakes. When you
have mixed the dough you may find
that, although you have carefully
followed the instructions, the dough
feels sticky and is difficult to work
with. Simply add a little more flour
and continue kneading. Repeat the
process until the dough is firm and
easy to model. Similarly, if it becomes
too dry, dampen your fingers and
smooth them over the dough.
Remember to keep sprinkling flour
over the work surface so that the
dough does not stick to it.

self-adhesive
stickers

AIR-DRIED CLAY

Traditionally, clay had to be hardened
in a kiln at a very high temperature.
This relatively new kind of clay, which
is sometimes called self-hardening

clay, contains fibers – so small you
cannot see them – that make it strong
as it dries out and eliminate the need
for baking. If you smooth over any
bumps and cracks with a damp finger
before the clay is dry, and give it two or
three coats of varnish when it has
hardened, you will be surprised at how
like china it looks. Take care, if you
drop it, it will break.

EDIBLE MATERIALS

We have used two kinds for our models
– marzipan and a store-bought mix
based on icing sugar.

Marzipan is delicious, but, if you can
resist eating it while you work, it can
be used for fruits, people and animals.
Vegetable food coloring can be added
to create a rainbow of shades, so you
could make a zoo full of exotic animals
or an aviary full of colored birds.

We used ready-mixed icing, which is
rolled out, to ice the cookies. If you add
peppermint essence to the mixture, you
will have peppermint creams, which
can be made doubly delicious if you
coat them in melted chocolate. You can
add vegetable food coloring to the
icing, or you could make a clown's face,
for example, in white icing and then
use food coloring to paint on the
features and decorations.

ruler

scissors

craft knife

craft glue

pencils

shells and sand

paper clips

string

dried plants

PAPIER MACHE

This is one of those materials that is always popular, although at the moment it is enjoying something of a revival. It is not expensive to make, and it can be used for all kinds of things – from toys and masks to plates and jewelry. You can use it in one of two ways. The easier method is to build up layers of pasted strips of paper – the more layers you use, the stronger the finished object will be. If you want to make something very large, you can make a base shape from something like Plasticine and apply pasted strips to the surface, or you can use a plate or a box in the same way. The other way is to make a squashy pulp using torn pieces of newspaper, glue, and water in a bowl. The pulp can be used to make more solid objects, such as the cat on page 47.

NATURAL MATERIALS

When you come back from a hike in the country or along the seashore, what do you do with all the pebbles, seedheads, shells, and nuts that you collect? Keep them safe in your "inspirations" box for those rainy days when you are at loose ends, and then let them inspire you to use them in all kinds of ways. Use them on their own to create imaginary land and seascapes, or combine them with another material, such as Plasticine, to make animals and birds.

winged paper clips

corks

BALSA WOOD

All the projects in this chapter are made with a soft, light wood called balsa wood, which you will find in your neighborhood hobby store. It can be easily cut with a craft knife – but do be careful. Ask an adult to help you while cutting out the wood. The best way to cut is to use four or five gentler cuts instead of making one strong, deep cut. This not only stops the wood from splintering but, more importantly, makes it less likely that you will cut your fingers. Use special adhesive for balsa wood (available from your hobby store) and use plain dressmaking pins to hold pieces together while the glue dries. If you enjoy making models with balsa wood, try making some boats that really sail, or airplanes that really fly, or some furniture for a dollhouse, all to your own designs.

driftwood

balsa wood

plants

pine cone

Plasticine

CHAPTER ONE
Oven-bake Clay

· · · · · · · · · · ·

Busy Bee Key Ring

Oven-bake clay is ideal for key rings because it is quite strong when it has been baked. You could make a pin or a brooch in the same way by gluing a brooch pin to the back of the baked shape. Think of other insects – a butterfly or ladybug, perhaps – to make with different colors.

YOU WILL NEED

- Oven-bake clay: yellow, black, white
- Toothpick
- Rolling pin
- Blunt knife
- Modeling tools
- Cookie sheet
- Clear varnish and brush
- Narrow yellow ribbon
- Key ring

1 Take a piece of yellow clay and smaller pieces of black and white clay. Roll the pieces in your hands to warm and soften them.

2 Roll the yellow clay into an egg shape with a point at one end and flatten the base by pressing it on the worktop.

3 Use the toothpick to make a hole in the pointed end – the tail – through which the ribbon for the key will be threaded later.

4 Roll out the black clay until it is about ⅛ inch thick, and **cut three strips, each about ¼ inch wide.**

5 Carefully position the strips on the bee's body, pressing them gently in place.

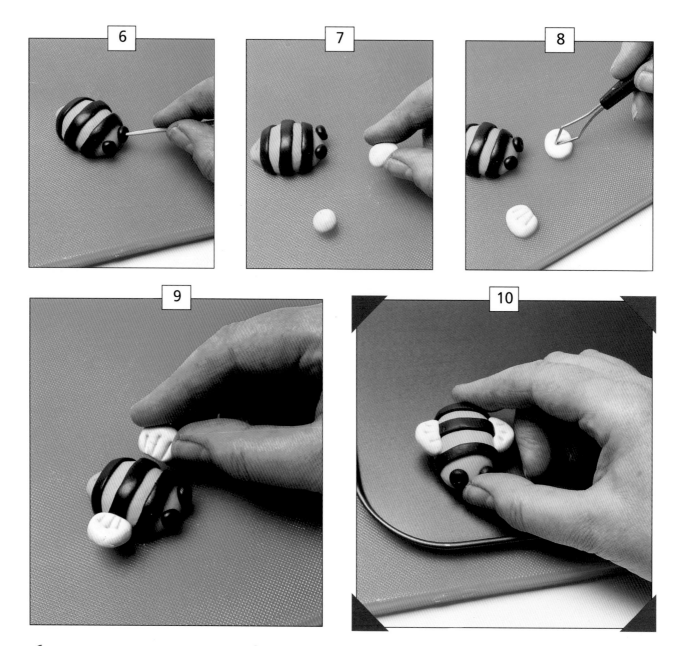

6 Roll the bits of black clay that are left together and make two small balls for the bee's eyes. Flatten them with your finger and press them into position with the toothpick.

7 Divide the white clay into two equal pieces and roll each piece into a flattened oval for the wings.

8 Use a modeling tool to mark three lines on each wing.

9 Press the wings onto the sides of the bee's body.

10 **Carefully place the bee on a cookie sheet and put it in the oven. Leave it to bake for 20-30 minutes at 265℉.**

SAFETY FIRST

☞ Some makes of oven-bake clays contain chemicals that may come off on your hands as you model with them. Always wash your hands carefully when you have finished working with clay, and never, never try to eat it!

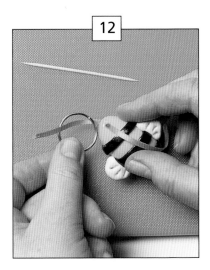

11 When the bee is cool, give it a coat of varnish. Remember to apply varnish to the base. Leave to dry.

12 Thread the ribbon through the hole in the tail and pull one end of the ribbon through the key ring.

13 Thread the ribbon through the hole again and tie a knot. Trim the ends of the ribbon.

Pirate Hat Magnet

This refrigerator magnet is in the shape of a pirate hat, but you could make a cowboy hat or a baseball cap in the same way. Some of the pieces used are very small, but if you use a toothpick or the end of a paper clip to help you, you should be able to move the little bits of clay around quite easily.

YOU WILL NEED

- Oven-bake clay: black, white
- Rolling pin
- White cardboard
- Pencil
- Scissors or craft knife
- Modeling tools
- Toothpick
- Cookie sheet
- Clear varnish and brush
- Small magnet
- Clear, all-purpose adhesive

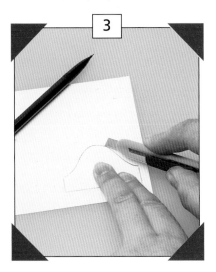

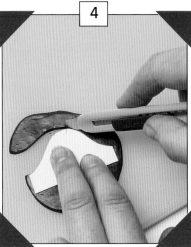

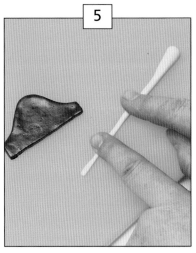

1 Warm and soften the black clay by rolling it between your hands.

2 Roll out the clay on your work top so that it is about ¼ inch thick.

3 Copy the hat template on page 90 and transfer the outline to a piece of white cardboard. **Cut out the shape of the hat from the cardboard.**

4 Place the hat shape on the black clay and carefully **cut around the cardboard.**

5 Take about half the white clay and soften it in your hands. Roll it on your work top to make a long, thin strip.

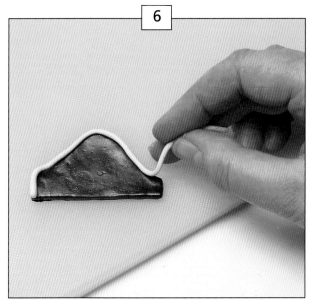

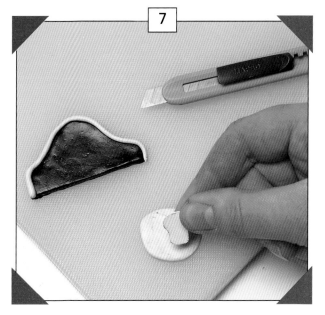

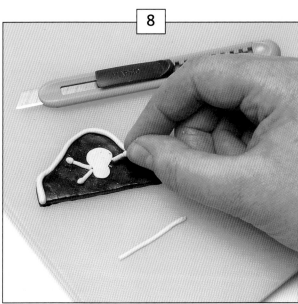

6 Place the white strip around the edge of the hat shape so that it looks like piping. Gently press it in place.

7 Copy the skull template on page 90 and transfer the outline to white cardboard. Roll out the remaining white clay until it is ⅛ inch thick. **Place the skull template on the clay and cut out the shape.**

8 Roll the bits of white clay together and form the clay into four sticks and four small balls. Press a ball at one end of each stick and use a toothpick to position the "bones" around the hat.

9 From the scraps of black clay, cut four small, thin strips for teeth and two tiny circles for eyes. Use a toothpick to position these on the skull. Use the toothpick to smooth and tidy up all the edges.

10 **Carefully place the hat on a cookie sheet and put it in the oven. Leave it to bake for 20–30 minutes at 265°F, or according to the manufacturer's instructions.**

11 When the hat is completely cool, apply a coat of varnish. Leave to dry.

12 Glue a small magnet to the back of the hat.

Pussycat Barrette

Hair clasps like this are easy to make and fun to wear. You could choose colors that will go with a favorite outfit or you could add some glitter for a party – some manufacturers of oven-bake clays also make glittery powders that can be added before baking. Metal barrettes are available from art and craft suppliers and beauty supply stores.

YOU WILL NEED

- Oven-bake clay: gray, white, black, yellow, pink
- Rolling pin
- Metal hair clasp
- Lipstick top
- Craft knife
- Toothpick
- Cookie sheet
- Clear varnish and brush

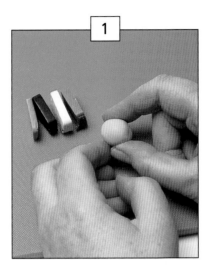

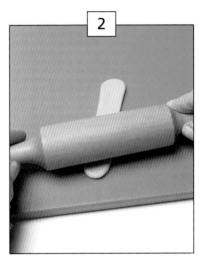

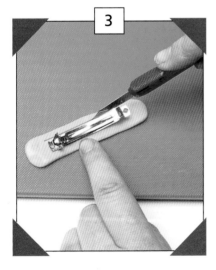

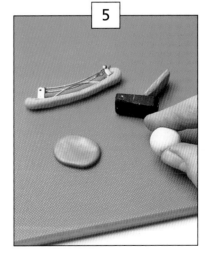

1 Soften the pieces of clay by rolling them in your hands. Roll the yellow clay into a ball.

2 Roll out the yellow clay into a long rectangle, about 2 x ½ inches.

3 Place the clasp face down on the yellow clay and **cut around the clasp so that the clay fits the top of the clasp.**

4 Press the clay to the top of the clasp. Make sure that the clay overlaps the ends of the clasp slightly.

5 Roll the gray, white, and black clay into balls and flatten each into a circle around ⅟₁₆ inch thick.

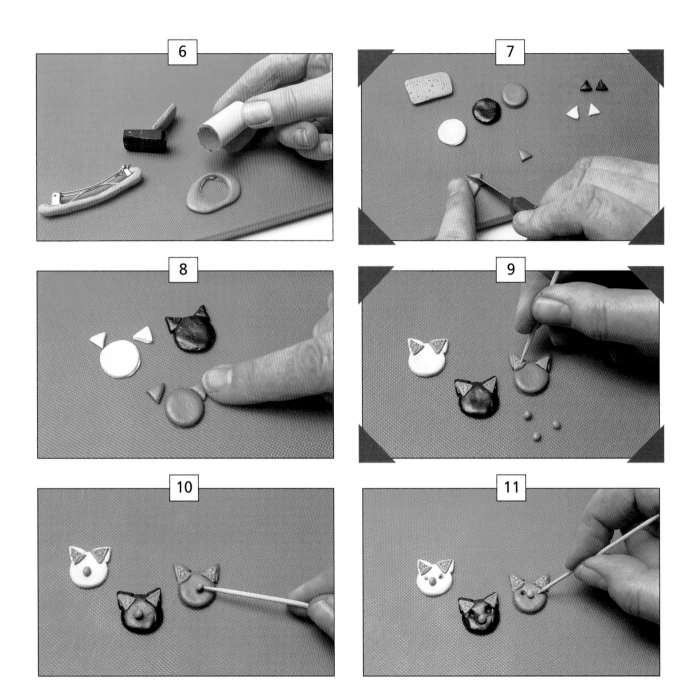

6 Use a small round object such as the top of a lipstick to press out neat circles for the cats' heads.

7 From the scraps of gray, white and black, **carefully cut two small triangles for the cats' ears – two gray, two white, and two black.**

8 Press the ears in place on the cats' heads.

9 Take a small piece of pink clay and soften it in your hands. Roll it out and **cut out six tiny triangles and three little balls.** Use a toothpick to make indentations in the ears, then carefully place the triangles in the ears.

10 Slightly flatten the balls and position them to form the cats' noses.

11 Blunt one end of a toothpick and use it to make indentations for the eyes on each face. Make sure that the hole goes all the way through so that the yellow background is visible.

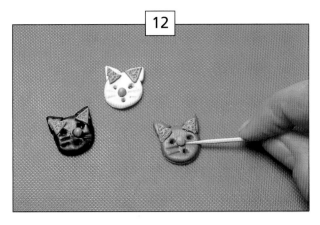

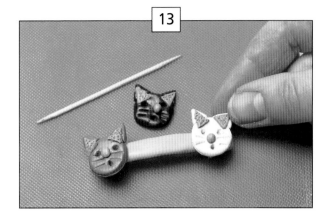

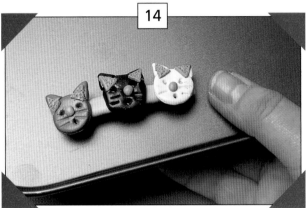

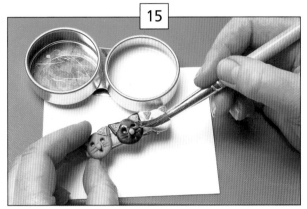

12 Use the sharp end of the toothpick to mark a hole for a mouth and lines for whiskers on each cat's face.

13 Place a cat at each end of the clasp and place one in the center, making sure that they are evenly spaced. Press them down very gently. The heat of the oven will make all the pieces stick together.

14 **Carefully place the clasp on a cookie sheet and put it in the oven. Leave it to bake for 20–30 minutes at 265°F or according to the manufacturer's instructions.**

15 When the clasp is cool, apply a coat of varnish. Leave to dry.

Multicolored Crayon Buttons

One of the exciting things about oven-bake clay is that there are so many colors available, which makes it the ideal material for these bright buttons. You could attach them to an old shirt or stitch them on a T-shirt for decoration. Alternatively, you could adapt the idea to make a brooch. You will need an adult to help with this project.

YOU WILL NEED

- Oven-bake clay: pink, orange, green, purple, turquoise, white
- Craft knife
- Toothpick
- Cookie sheet
- Clear varnish and brush

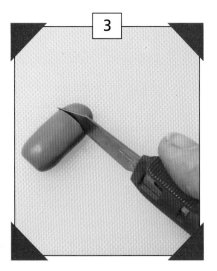

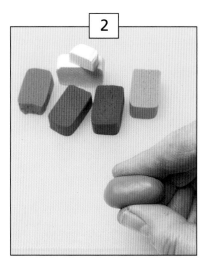

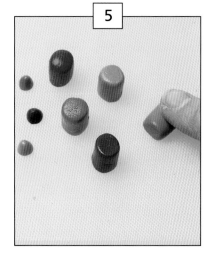

1 **Cut pieces measuring of each color.** You will need slightly more white.

2 Working each color except the white in turn, warm and soften the clay by rolling it in your hands.

3 **Cut off the end of each tube and put the little pieces to one side.**

4 Shape one of the little pieces of each color into a point, like a pencil.

5 Roll the large pieces of colored clay into pencil shapes. Press each one gently on your work top to flatten the base.

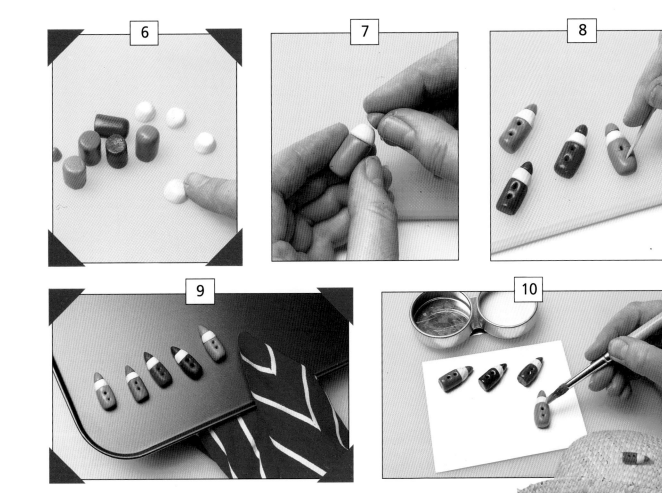

6 Soften the white clay and roll it into a tube. **Cut it into five equal lengths** and mold each piece into a cone shape with a flat top.

7 Put each "crayon" together, with the little colored tops matching the larger sections.

8 Use a toothpick to make two holes in the main part of each pencil. Make sure that the holes go right through to the other side.

9 **Carefully place the buttons on a cookie sheet and put it in the oven. Leave it to bake for 20–30 minutes at 265°F, or according to the manufacturer's instructions.**

10 When the buttons are completely cool, apply varnish to both sides and leave to dry.

CHAPTER TWO
Salt Dough
· · · · · · · · · · ·

Blast-off!

These Christmas tree decorations can be as simple or as complex as you want. You can add patterns by painting more details or by using more colors, or you can leave them plain. We have made a space rocket, but you could use pastry cutters to make some interesting shapes, or you can create animals or flowers freehand.

YOU WILL NEED

- Large mixing bowl
- Mixing spoon
- 2 cups all-purpose flour
- 1 cup salt
- 1 cup water
- 1 tablespoon oil
- White cardboard
- Scissors and craft knife
- Rolling pin
- Modeling tools
- Toothpick
- Paints: white, red, blue, silver, black
- Paintbrushes
- Varnish and brush
- Cord or narrow ribbon

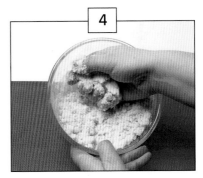

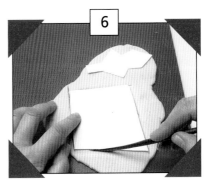

1 Add the flour to the salt in a large bowl.

2 Carefully pour in the water, adding a little at a time and stirring it with a large mixing spoon.

3 Add the oil and stir it in.

4 Knead the mixture with your fingers until the dough begins to hold together. Continue to knead until it becomes smooth.

5 Copy from the template on page 90 and transfer the outlines to white cardboard. Cut out the shapes.

6 Roll the dough until it is about ¼ inch thick. Place the templates on the dough and **cut out shapes.**

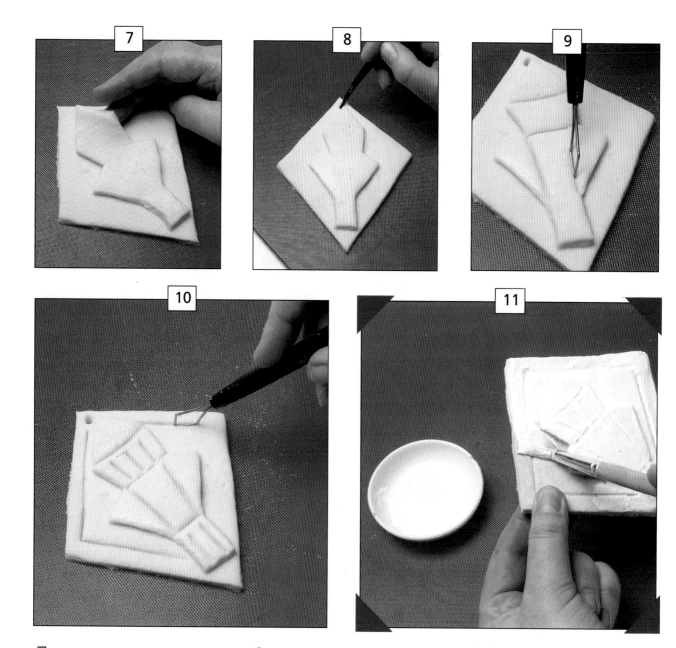

7 Brush a little water over the central part of the diamond shape and place the rocket shape on the diamond, making sure that there is an equal space all around.

8 Use a cocktail stick, modeling tool, or toothpick to make a hole in what will be the top of the diamond.

9 Use a modeling tool to mark the fins and tail of the rocket.

10 Mark a pattern of lines on the top and base of the rocket and use the modeling tool to impress a border around the edge of the diamond.

11 Allow the decoration to dry naturally **or ask an adult to help you bake it for about 8 hours at 250°F**. When it is completely dry or cool, apply a white undercoat all over the surface.

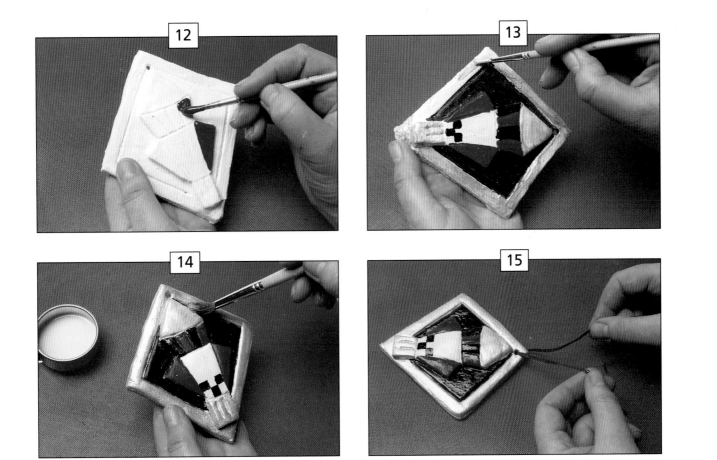

12 When the undercoat is dry, paint the fins and sections of the top red. Paint the background area inside the border dark blue. Use black paint to add details and patterns to the rocket. If necessary, go over the body of the rocket with white paint to cover all the smudges and uneven lines.

13 Paint the border of the diamond and the top and bottom of the rocket silver.

14 When the paint is completely dry, if you want, apply a coat or two of varnish to protect the paint and to give the decoration a good glossy finish.

15 When the varnish is dry, thread a piece of cord or narrow ribbon through the hole in the top so that you can hang up the decoration.

Clucking Egg Cup

This egg cup is made from a single piece of dough with the decoration added using modeling tools and paints. Use an egg to check the size of the cup – a hard-boiled one, preferably – and leave the egg in the cup for a day or two, because the dough will shrink slightly as it dries.

YOU WILL NEED

- Mixing bowl and spoon
- 2 cups all-purpose flour
- 1 cup salt
- 1 cup water
- 1 tablespoon oil
- Blunt knife
- Egg (hard-boiled)
- Modeling tools
- Paints: white, yellow, red, black
- Paintbrushes
- Varnish and brush

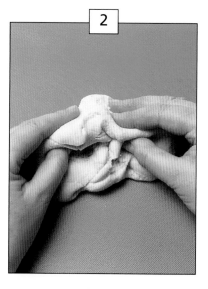

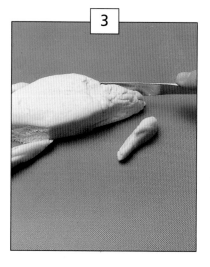

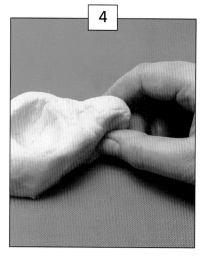

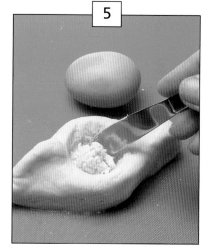

1 Add the flour to the salt in a large bowl. Carefully pour in the water, adding a little at a time and stirring it with a wooden spoon. Add the oil and stir it in. Knead the mixture with your fingers until the dough begins to hold together.

2 Turn out the dough onto a lightly floured surface and continue to knead it until it is smooth.

3 Use a blunt knife to cut off a piece about 3 x 2 inches and trim off the corners to make it into a rough diamond shape.

4 Begin to mold the dough with your fingers, pinching it at the head and tail ends and pressing a hole in the center for the egg.

5 Use a blunt knife to dig out a hole for the egg in the center.

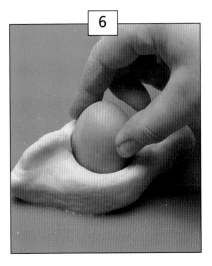

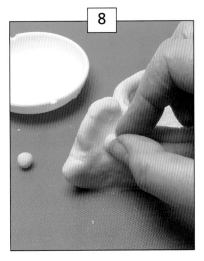

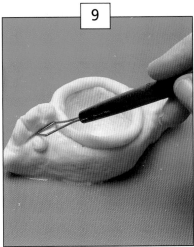

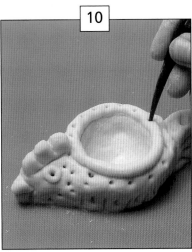

6 Check the size of the hole with an egg and smooth over the surface of the egg cup with your fingers.

7 Roll out a tube of dough and place it around the rim of the hole, using a little water to make the dough stick.

8 Take a little more dough and roll out two small balls. Press them to the sides of the chicken's head for the eyes.

9 Use a modeling tool to begin to mark the features on the chicken's face. Remember to mark a line along the beak to show where it would open. Add some marks to the tail to decorate the surface of the dough.

10 Use the handle of a paintbrush to indent a series of dots all over the surface of the dough, including the rim around the egg holder.

11 Allow the egg cup to dry naturally **or ask an adult to help you bake it for about 8 hours at 250°F**. When the egg cup is completely dry or cool, apply a white undercoat all over the surface.

TIP

☛ While you are working, check from time to time that the egg still fits inside the hole. Put the egg into the egg cup and gently move it back and forth to increase the hole size.

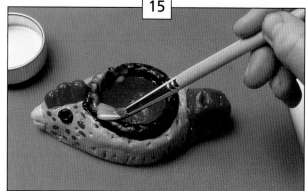

12 Mix some orange paint (red and yellow) and paint the chicken's body.

13 Paint the comb and tail red and add some red dots on the sides of the face. Paint the inside of the egg cup red.

14 Paint the rim around the top of the egg cup black. Paint the beak yellow and leave all the paint to dry.

15 Apply at least two coats of varnish, allowing the first coat to dry before you apply the next. You must also remember to apply varnish to the base of the egg cup.

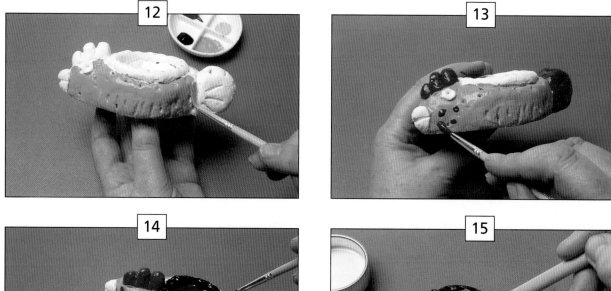

> ### TIP
>
> ☛ The more coats of varnish you apply, the more waterproof the egg cup will be. However, it is probably not a good idea to immerse it in water, so when you have used it, wipe it gently with a damp cloth.

Dish of Moon and Stars

This highly decorated plate is the most difficult of the salt dough projects because it is delicate to handle. Although the decoration looks complex, it is quite simple to apply. It would look attractive hanging on a wall, so you could make a hanger from a paper clip, glued securely to the back of the plate when you have finished.

YOU WILL NEED

- Mixing bowl and spoon
- 2 cups all-purpose flour
- 1 cup salt
- 1 cup water
- 1 tablespoon oil
- Large mixing bowl
- Large rolling pin
- Petroleum jelly
- Ovenproof plate
- Blunt knife
- Ruler
- Pastry brush
- Cookie cutters (star-shaped and round)
- Pen top
- Modeling tools
- Paints: white, blue, black, silver
- Paintbrushes
- Varnish and brush

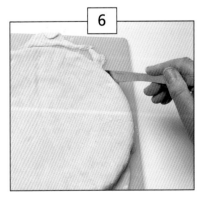

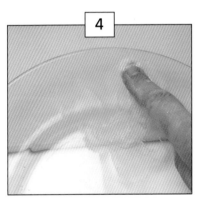

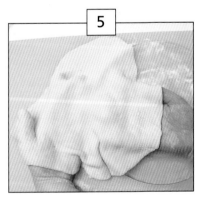

1 Add the flour to the salt in a large bowl. Carefully pour in the water, adding a little at a time and stirring it with a mixing spoon. Add the oil and stir it in.

2 Knead the mixture with your fingers until the dough begins to hold together. Continue to knead until smooth.

3 Lightly flour your worktop and roll out the dough until it is about ¼ inch thick.

4 Smear a layer of petroleum jelly over the surface of the ovenproof plate.

5 Carefully lift the dough and place it over the plate.

6 Press the dough gently down over the plate, taking care that you do not flatten it too much. Trim off the edge neatly all round with a blunt knife.

7 Roll out the scraps of dough again and use a ruler to cut strips about ½ inch wide.

8 Use a brush to dampen the edge of the dough and press the border in place all the way round. Use your fingers to smooth the joins in the dough strips.

9 Roll out some more dough so that it is less than ¼ inch thick. Use a small star-shaped cookie cutter to cut out nine stars. Cut one star with a larger cutter.

10 Use the side of a round cookie cutter to cut out some crescent moon shapes.

11 Brush the surface of the dough lightly with water so that the decorations will stick in place, then put the large star in the center of the plate. Arrange eight of the small stars and the moons around the edge of the plate, and place the last small star in the center of the large one.

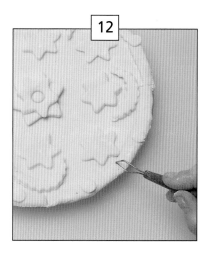

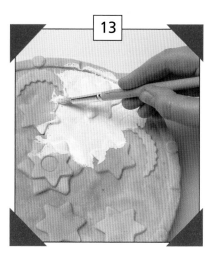

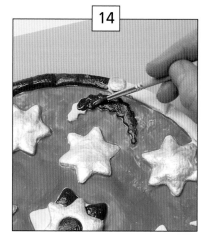

14 Leave the dough plate on the ovenproof plate while you decorate it so that it does not crack. Paint the background blue and paint the stars and circles silver. Mix dark blue (blue and black) to paint the edge, the moons, and the large star in the center and the circle in the center. Apply two coats of paint to give a really deep blue.

15 When the paint is dry, carefully remove the plate from the ovenproof plate and apply at least two coats of varnish, remembering to allow the first coat to dry before you apply the next.

12 Use the top of a large pen or something similar to cut out eight small circles from the dough and arrange them evenly around the rim of the plate. Use the pen top to impress a circle in the middle of the central star. Use a modeling tool to make a pattern of indentations between each circle. Pressing the edging down will also help make it stick to the dough underneath.

13 **Ask an adult to help you bake the plate for about 8 hours at 250°F.** When the plate is cool, apply a white undercoat all over the surface.

Air-dried Clay

· · · · · · · · · · ·

Rainbow Pencil Holder

It is possible to use this method to make all kinds of shapes and sizes. If you prefer, you can make a shallow pot with a matching lid. Because this is designed as a pencil holder, it is pretty tall. You could paint it to match other things on your desk or you could decorate it with a pattern of spots or stripes.

YOU WILL NEED

- Air-dried clay
- Rolling pin
- Jam jar or mug
- Blunt knife
- Paints: white and colors of your choice
- Paintbrushes
- Varnish and brushes

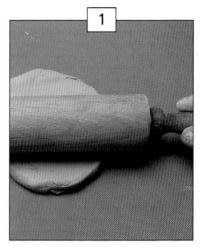

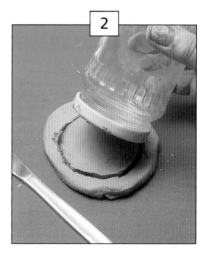

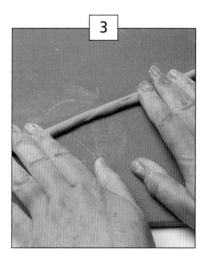

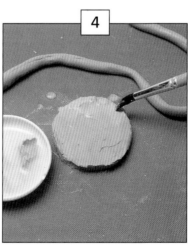

1 Take a piece of clay about 3 x 2 inches and roll it in your hands to soften it. Then roll it out on your worktop until it is about ¼ inch thick.

2 Find a jar or mug that is about the size you want the finished pot to be. Press it on the clay and cut around it to make the base of the pot.

3 Take pieces of clay and roll them into lengths just over ¼ inch thick. Make sure they are smooth and even.

4 Using some wet clay as a kind of glue, begin to coil the strips on the base. The wet clay will help the clay coils to stick together.

5 Keep adding spirals of clay until the pot is the height you want. Do not worry if it does not look very even – when it is painted no one will notice. Roll two thicker pieces of clay. Coil one of these thick pieces around the base of the pot. As well as making the pot look more interesting, it will help to make it more stable.

6

7

8

9

6 Coil the other thick piece around the rim of the pot, placing it so that it sticks out a little and balances the coil around the base. Check that the pot is straight and leave to dry

7 When the pot is completely dry, paint it white all over.

Leave to dry. This pot is painted in a rainbow of colors, but you could use just one or two colors if preferred. If you want to use purple, mix blue and red together.

8 Mix some dark blue (blue and black) to paint the inside of the pot.

9 When the paint is completely dry, apply a coat of varnish to the inside and outside of the pot. Leave to dry.

TIP

☛ If the clay gets too dry while you are working with it, dampen it with a little water and smooth over the cracks.

Bluebird Candlestick

This kind of clay is excellent for making the kinds of objects you would normally see made from ceramics, because when it has hardened it looks as if it has been baked in a kiln. This candlestick is easy to make. It is mostly cut from one piece of clay and then molded into shape. Try making a matching pair of candlesticks.

YOU WILL NEED
- White cardboard
- Pencil
- Scissors
- Air-dried clay
- Blunt knife
- Candle
- Modeling tools
- Paints: white, blue, orange, black, turquoise
- Paintbrushes
- Varnish and brush

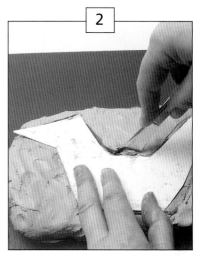

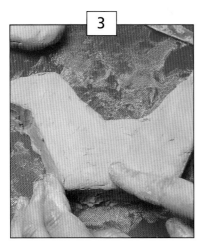

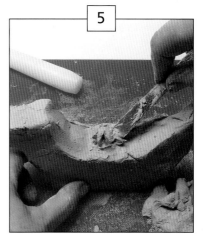

1 Copy the template from page 90 and transfer the outline to white cardboard. Cut out the shape of the bird from the cardboard.

2 Take a piece of clay, about 9 x 5 x 1¼ inches, and place the template on it. Cut around the outline of the bird. Put the remnants of clay in a plastic bag, except for a bit that is about the size of an ordinary egg, which you will need for the wings and eyes.

3 Smooth the edges of the clay with your fingers.

4 Trim the edges from the beak and tail of the bird so that they form points. Smooth the edges again.

5 With the bird sitting on your worktop, use a candle to mark the position of the hole in the back. Use a blunt knife to make the hole deeper, then smooth the surface neatly with your fingers.

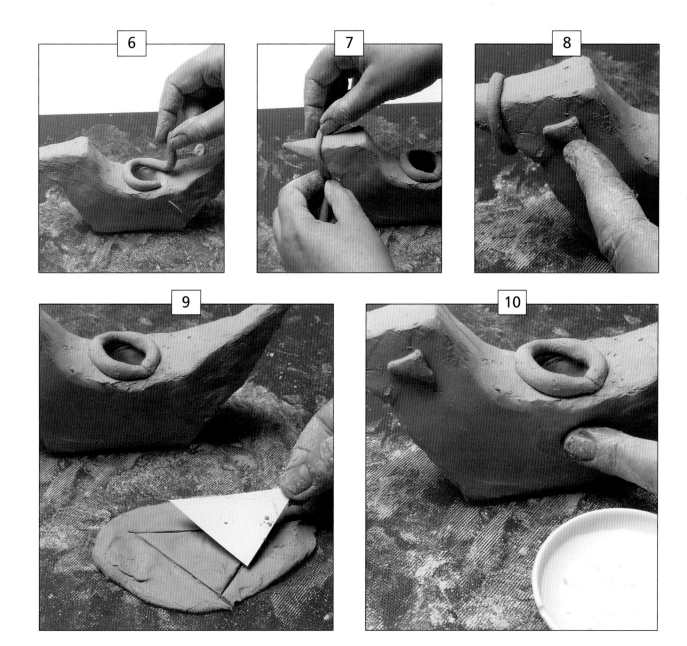

6 Roll out a piece of clay about ¼ inch thick and place it around the hole.

7 Place another piece of rolled-out clay around the beak. Smooth the joins with your fingers.

8 Flatten some of the remaining clay until it is about ⅛ inch thick and cut two triangles, each about ½ inch along each side, for the eyes. Press them in position on the sides of the head, sticking them down with a little water.

9 Cut two large triangles from the remaining clay, each triangle about 1½ inch along each side. Make a template from cardboard to help you.

10 Apply a little water to the side of the bird where the wings will go. You may find that scratching the surface of the clay helps makes the wings stick to the body more easily.

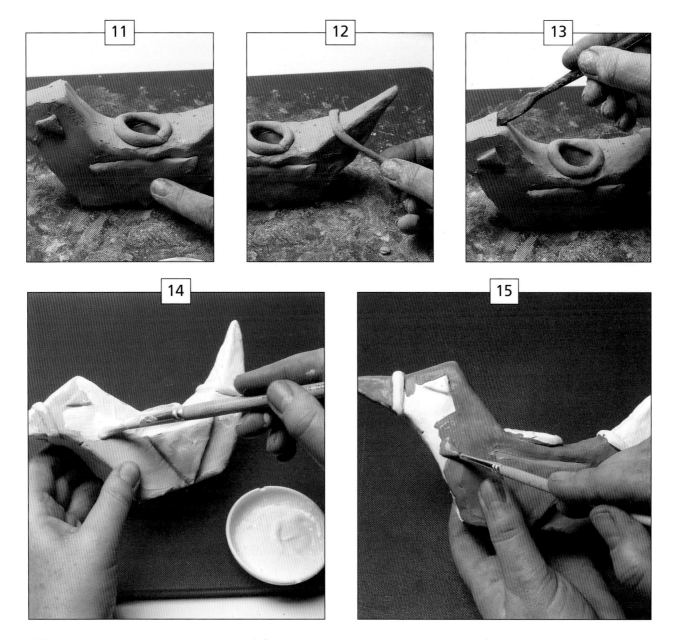

11 Press the wings into place, arranging them so that both sides match. Smooth over the top edges carefully with your fingers.

12 Use the remaining clay to make a little roll to go around the tail, matching the roll you put around the beak.

13 Smooth over the hole surface with a modeling tool, then leave the clay to dry.

14 Apply a coat of white paint all over the candlestick and leave to dry.

15 Paint the wings and beak orange and the body blue or turquoise. Leave the eyes white.

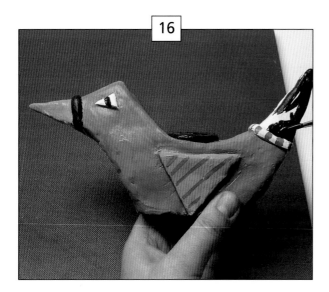

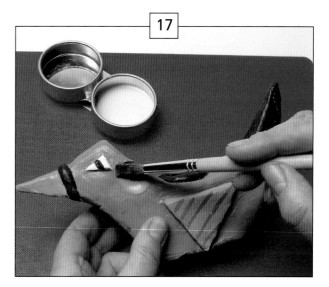

16 Use dark blue (blue and black) for the tail, the hole for the candle, and the rings around the beak and tail. Add blue stripes on the wings, and add some white decoration around the tail.

17 When the paint is dry, apply at least two coats of varnish to the whole surface, making sure that the first coat is dry before you apply the second.

Metallic Marine Brooch

Although this is much smaller than the candlestick and the pencil holder, it is not difficult to make, as long as you have nimble fingers and use modeling tools to decorate the surface. Jewelry is always fun to make, because you can decorate it with all kinds of small stones and beads.

YOU WILL NEED

- Air-dried clay
- Rolling pin
- White cardboard
- Pencil
- Scissors
- Blunt knife
- Modeling tools
- Toothpick
- Paints: white, light blue, dark blue, silver
- Paintbrushes
- Varnish and brush
- Brooch back
- Clear, all-purpose adhesive

1

2
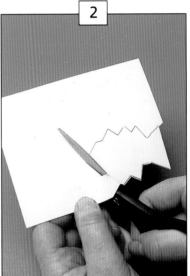

3

4
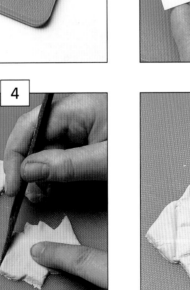

5

1 Roll out a piece of clay so that it is about ¼ inch thick.

2 Copy the fish template from page 90 and transfer the outline to white cardboard. Cut it out.

3 Place the cardboard shape on the clay and **use a craft knife or a kitchen knife to cut around the outline**.

4 Use a blade of a knife or your fingers to smooth the edge of the fish.

5 Use a modeling tool to draw lines to represent the fish's fins and add other decoration as you wish. Make a hole for the fish's eye with a wooden toothpick.

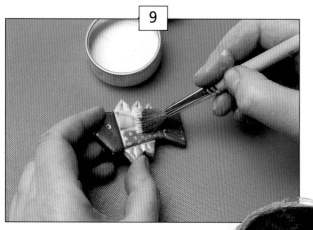

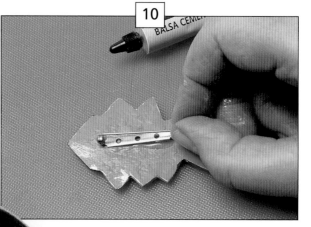

6 Leave the fish to dry, then turn it over so that the back can dry. If necessary, fill any holes by running wet clay over the surface and carefully smoothing it over to give a good finish.

7 Paint the fish, beginning with a light blue. If you mix silver with the blue, you will get lovely metallic, shimmery colors. Use darker blue for the head and tail.

8 Paint the fins silver and paint the back of the fish pale blue.

9 When the paint is dry, apply a coat of varnish all over the fish. Allow the varnish to dry.

10 Glue the brooch pin to the back of the fish and leave the glue to set hard before wearing the brooch.

Circles Vase

This vase is more highly decorated than the pencil holder, and it is more complicated to make. Unlike clay that is fired in a kiln, air-dried clay is not waterproof, and if you want to make a vase in which you can place flowers, you need to put a glass jar, slightly smaller than the vase, inside for the water. Alternatively, use it to hold a pretty display of dried flowers and grasses.

YOU WILL NEED

- Glass jar and plastic bag
- Petroleum jelly
- Air-dried clay
- Rolling pin
- Blunt knife
- Cookie cutter or similar, about 1¼ inch across
- Pen top or smaller circular object
- Paints: white, yellow, blue (or turquoise), red, black
- Paintbrushes
- Varnish and brush

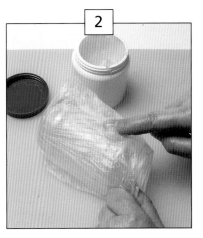

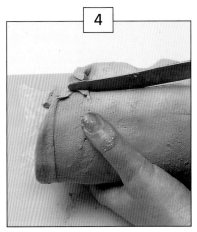

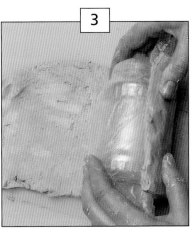

TIP

☞ If you do not succeed in finishing the vase in one day, keep the clay soft and workable by covering it with a damp cloth.

---

1 Place the glass jar inside a plastic bag.

2 Cover the bag with a layer of petroleum jelly.

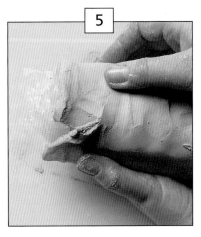

3 Roll out the clay until it is about ¼ inch thick and long enough to go right round the jar. Wrap the clay around the jar.

4 Trim away any excess clay.

5 Smooth the join with your fingers.

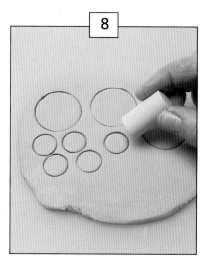

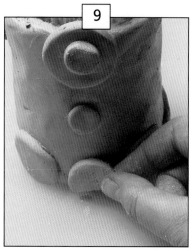

6 Stand the jar on a piece of the remaining rolled-out clay and with a knife cut around the bottom edge. Smooth the join with your fingers to give a neat finish.

7 Measure up about 4½ inches from the bottom and use a ruler to mark a line right around the vase. Cut off the top.

8 Roll out some of the trimmings of clay that are left until they are about ⅛ inch thick. Use the cookie cutter to cut out 10 circles. Use the pen top or a similar object to cut out 12 circles.

9 Use a piece of wet clay to stick larger circles around the top and bottom of the vase. Stick small circles in the center and put some small circles around the center. Cut two of the larger circles in half and position them between the circles around the bottom of the vase.

10 Place some small circles between the large circles around the top of the vase. Use the handle of a paintbrush to make indentations in the centers of some of the circles and to make a series of evenly spaced holes around the top edge of the vase.

11 Allow the vase to dry. When it is completely dry, remove the glass jar from the inside by pulling on the plastic bag.

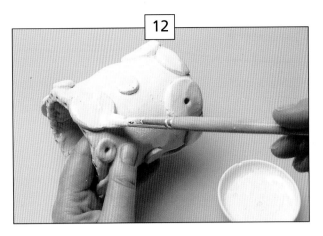

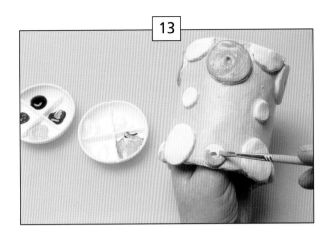

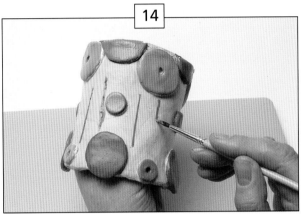

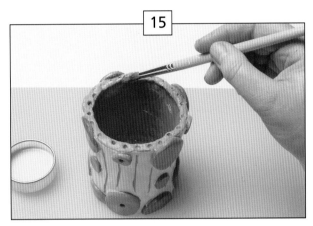

12 Apply a coat of white paint to the whole surface of the vase. Leave it to dry.

13 Paint the vase yellow all over. Allow the yellow to dry before using a pale blue (dark blue and white) or turquoise to paint some of the circles

.

14 Mix pink (red and white) and use it to paint some stripes down the vase, then use purple (red and blue) to paint some of the other circles. Leave the paint to dry.

15 Apply varnish all over the vase, inside and out and leave to dry.

CHAPTER FOUR
Papier Mâché

Good-luck Cat

Papier mâché is French for "mashed paper" and it is made very simply from newspaper mixed with water and wallpaper paste. Strips of paper can be used, but for this project we are going to use a paper pulp, which is quick to make but takes quite a long time to dry out. The whiskers give the cat a wonderfully life-like look – almost as if it is about to catch a mouse.

YOU WILL NEED

- 2–3 newspapers
- 1 cup water and 1 rounded tablespoon wallpaper paste
- Large mixing bowl
- Modeling tools
- Paints: white, black, red, green
- Paintbrushes
- Pencil
- Toothpick
- 6 whiskers (from a broom or brush)
- Clear, all-purpose adhesive
- Plaid ribbon and bell

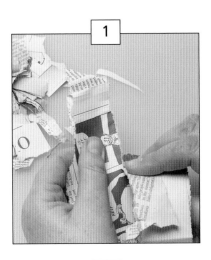

1 Tear some newspaper into small pieces. Try to make the pieces more or less the same size.

2 Add the wallpaper paste to the water in a large bowl and mix them together well. Leave the paste to stand for a while until the paste begins to thicken.

3 Add the pieces of paper to the paste, mixing them well. Keep on adding paper until the paste has all been soaked up.

4 Squeeze the paper and paste mix in your hands to remove excess water. then place it on your worktop. You need a lump that is about 6 inches thick and 4½ inches wide.

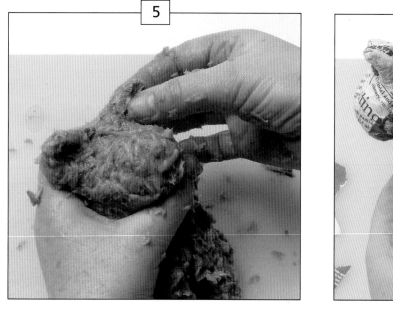

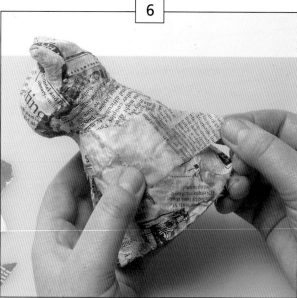

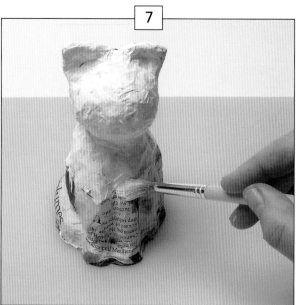

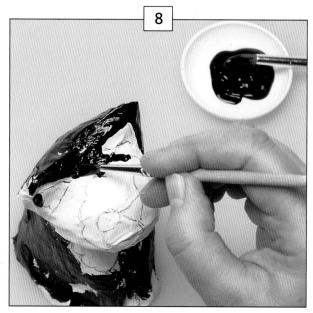

5 Begin to model the pulp into the shape of a cat, modeling the head and ears. If the pulp is too wet, add a little more paper or leave it to dry for a while in a warm, dry room.

6 Squeeze the pulp between your fingers to create the details and use a modeling tool to define

the front legs and the tail. Apply little pieces of paper to the surface to give a smooth finish.

7 Place the cat in a warm, dry place – near a radiator, for example – and leave it to dry. When it is completely dry, apply a coat of white paint to cover the newsprint completely.

8 Use a pencil to draw the eyes, nose, paws, and chest on the cat. Paint the body and top of the head black. Use pink (red and white) for inside the ears and the nose, and paint the eyes green.

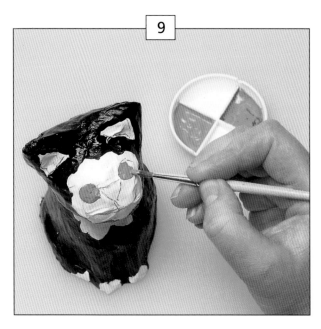

11 Finish off your cat by fastening a ribbon and bell around its neck.

9 Use black paint to add a fine line around the nose and eyes, and paint in the line of the mouth.

10 Use a toothpick to make three holes at each side of the cat's face. Dip the end of each bristle into glue and insert it into a hole to form a whisker.

Dinosaur Mobile

These dinosaurs are made from pieces of card that have been covered with strips of paper to give texture so that they look as if they have thick, scaly, dinosaur-type skin. You can cover both sides of each dinosaur or, for speed, just decorate one side. The string is attached to each shape by a colored paper clip.

YOU WILL NEED

- White card
- Pencil
- Scissors
- Cardboard
- Craft knife (optional)
- Newspaper
- 1 rounded tablespoon wallpaper paste and 1 cup water
- Paintbrushes
- Paints: white, black, and colors of your choice
- Toothpick
- Colored paper clips
- Clear, all-purpose adhesive
- Varnish and brush
- Strong black thread

1 Transfer the templates on pages 92–93 to white card and cut around the outlines.

2 Place the templates on the cardboard and draw around the outlines. **Cut out the shapes of the dinosaurs.** If you **use a craft knife, ask an adult to help, because the cardboard can be difficult to cut through.**

3 Tear small rectangles from the newspaper and soak them in mixed wallpaper paste. Cover the cardboard shapes with pieces of paper. You only need apply one layer to each side and there is no need to be too neat because you want to give a rough look to the finished dinosaur.

4 Leave the paste to dry, then decide if you want to decorate the other side. If so, repeat the previous step. When the dinosaur is completely dry, apply a coat of white paint to cover all the newsprint.

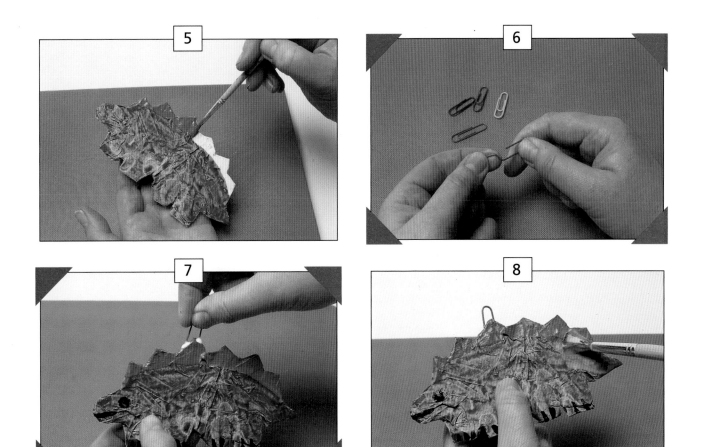

5 When the paint is dry, decorate the dinosaurs in colors of your choice. We used green and purple for the Brontosaurus. Don't forget to cover and paint the main section of the mobile. Use black paint to add eyes to the dinosaurs.

6 Ask an adult to help you unbend a paper clip. Take care, because the ends can be sharp.

7 Make two holes in the top of each dinosaur with a toothpick or something similar. Thread the paper clip through the holes, holding it firm with a tiny blob of glue.

8 When you have threaded paper clips through the tops of all the dinosaurs, varnish each shape. If you have decorated both sides, allow the varnish to dry on one side before turning it over to varnish the other side.

9 Attach a paper clip to each of the four corners of the main piece of the mobile. Add one in the center.

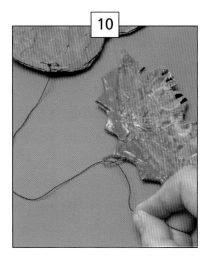

10 Thread lengths of cotton through each of the hooks on the main section of the mobile and attach dinosaurs to each one.

11 Bend under the ends of the legs of the dinosaur to go on top of the mobile. Use strong adhesive to glue it to the center of the top of the main piece. The mobile can be suspended by means of a thread attached to the hook in the top of this brontosaurus, or tied around the dinosaur and threaded through the hook in the center of the leaf.

TIP

☛ Don't tie the thread too tightly at first. Experiment with different lengths of thread until you are satisfied that the mobile is properly balanced, then tie securely in place. The longer the piece of thread, the "heavier" the object suspended from it will seem to be.

Treasure Chest

When you have completed this chest, you could make it extra secure by adding a small padlock to it, so that you can keep your special treasures in it. It is simply made from an ordinary cardboard box – one that contained chocolates or tea bags, for example – but the layers of papier mâché make it sturdy and stable.

YOU WILL NEED

- 1 rounded tablespoon wallpaper paste and 1 cup of water
- Bowl
- Newspaper
- Cardboard box
- Paints: white, red
- Paintbrushes
- Ruler
- Black construction paper
- Scissors
- Craft glue and brush
- Toothpick
- Approximately 43 winged paper clips
- Varnish and brush
- Screw-in eyes (optional)
- Small padlock (optional)

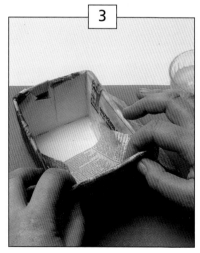

1 Mix the wallpaper paste and water in a large bowl and tear pieces of newspaper to fit the sides of the box. Paste pieces of newspaper to the sides. You can either dip the newspaper in the paste or apply the paste with a brush.

2 Cover the sides, base and top of the box with about six layers of paper.

3 Make sure that you take the newspaper strips over the sides of the box to make a neat edge.

4 Leave the box in a warm, dry room until it is completely dry, then give it a coat of white paint to cover all the newsprint.

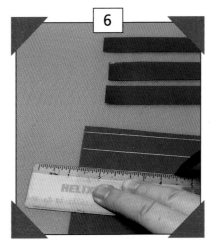

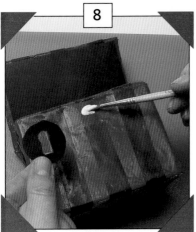

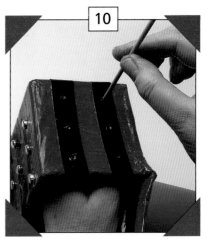

5 When the white undercoat is dry, paint the box red.

6 Use a ruler to measure three strips of black paper. Each strip should be about ¾ inch wide and be long enough to go all the way over the lid and down the back of the box. Measure and cut seven shorter strips, the same width, that are slightly longer than the depth of the box. Trim about 1 inch from one of these strips. **If you use a craft knife to cut the paper, ask an adult to help.**

7 Use craft glue to stick the black strips around the box. Put one at each end and one in the middle. Make sure that the strips are long enough to tuck inside the lid and under the box at the back so that there are no rough edges.

8 Stick the shorter strips to the sides and front of the box, bending the ends neatly under the box and in along the top edge. The shortest strip goes in the center of the front. Cover the ends by sticking a piece of black paper over the inside of the lid. **Cut a circle of black paper, about 1¼ inches across, and cut out**

the shape of a keyhole in the center. Ask an adult to help you cut out the outline. Glue the keyhole to the center front of the box.

9 Apply a coat of watered-down craft glue to the outside of the box.

10 When the glue is dry, **use a toothpick or something similar to pierce a series of holes, about 1¼ inches apart, along the black strips.** Ask an adult to help if the card and paper are now too thick to be easily pierced.

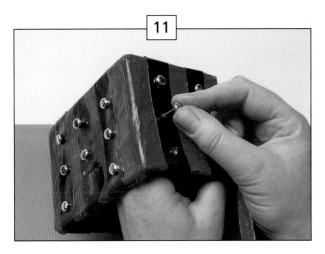

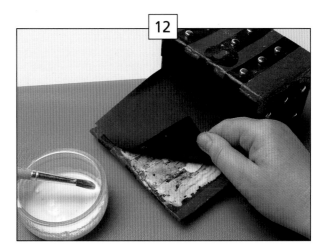

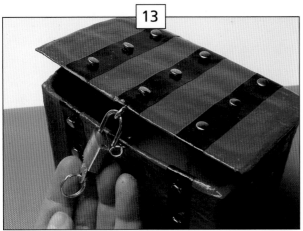

13 If you wish, screw two small round-headed screws into the lid and into the center front of the box. Finish off your box with a small padlock.

11 Insert a paper clip through each of the holes, opening out the wings on the inside.

12 Cut pieces of black paper to cover the inside of the box. Use plenty of glue to make sure that the paper is firmly glued over the opened-out paper clips. Apply a coat of varnish, but take care that you do not varnish the heads of the paper clips.

Dancing Doll

Even though this little doll is wearing clothes, no sewing is necessary. The material is held in place with adhesive and double-sided adhesive tape. The doll is made from bits and pieces that would normally be thrown away. Part of the fun of using these scraps is to make something that looks professionally made, which even has moving legs and arms.

YOU WILL NEED

- 1 rounded tablespoon wallpaper paste and 1 cup water
- Large bowl
- Scissors
- Newspaper
- 2 drinking straws
- Cardboard tube (from inside of toilet paper)
- Masking tape
- Knitting needle
- String
- Paints: white, red, blue, brown
- Paintbrushes
- Black construction paper
- Craft glue
- Double-sided adhesive tape
- Blue and red check fabric, about 6 x 18 inches
- Red rickrack braid
- 3 blue buttons

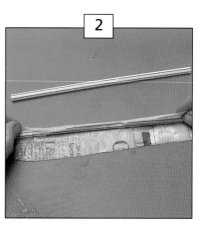

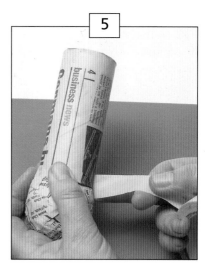

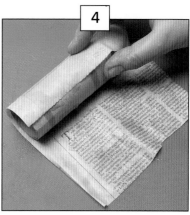

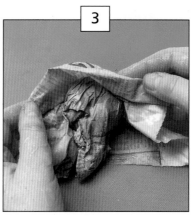

1 Mix the wallpaper paste and water in a bowl and let stand for a while until the paste thickens.

2 Cut two strips of newspaper to fit around the straws. Dip the newspaper in the paste and roll up each straw in a piece of newspaper.

3 Ball up a piece of newspaper to form the doll's head, making sure there is a neck, and dip into the paste. Cover the head and neck with paper to give a smooth finish.

4 Cover the tube with a piece of pasted newspaper and leave it to dry.

5 Use masking tape to hold the head in one end of the tube. When the straws are dry, cut each one in half.

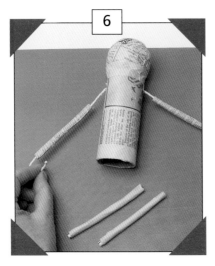

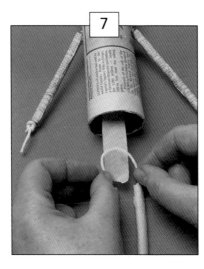

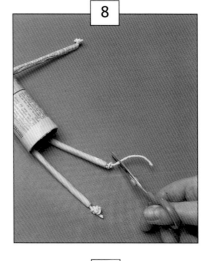

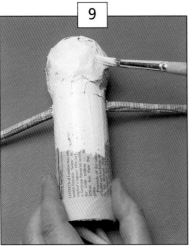

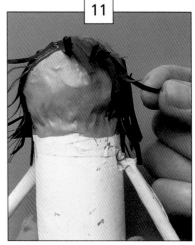

6 **Use a knitting needle to make two holes in the top of the tube, a short distance from the head. Ask an adult to help you thread a length of string through the holes and to thread a piece of straw onto the string to represent arms.** Make sure the string is loose enough for the arms to hang, then tie a knot in each end.

7 Thread a piece of string through the other two pieces of straw. Attach the string inside the tube, holding it in place with a piece of masking tape. Press the masking tape firmly inside the tube.

8 Tie knots in the end of the string to prevent the "legs" from slipping off and then trim the ends.

9 Paint the head and upper body of the doll with white paint to cover all the newsprint. Paint the head a pale brown color.

10 **Cut the black paper into bangs. Ask an adult to help, because this will look better if you can make fine, even bangs.** Use craft glue to glue on the strips of black bangs to look like hair.

11 Trim the black bangs to length. Gently tease out bits of the black bangs to make them resemble curls and waves.

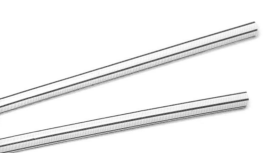

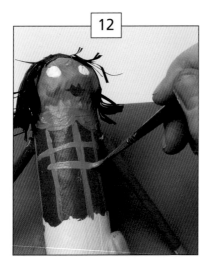

12 Paint the features on the doll's face, including pink cheeks. Paint the upper body and arms of the doll red. Use blue paint to make a pattern of checks and squares on the doll's body, matching the blue

of the material you will be using for the skirt as closely as possible. Add a black dot for the pupil in the middle of the doll's eyes.

13 Use double-sided tape to turn under one of the long edges of the skirt fabric to make a hem.

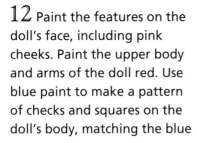

14 Put a piece of double-sided tape around the doll's waist. Gather the unhemmed edge of the skirt fabric and arrange it around the doll, sticking it to the tape.

15 Stick a second piece of double-sided tape around the doll's waist, this time on top of the gathered skirt. Press a piece of rickrack braid around the waist so that it looks like a belt. Stick another piece around the neck. Stick three little buttons down the front of doll's body.

CHAPTER FIVE

Edible Materials

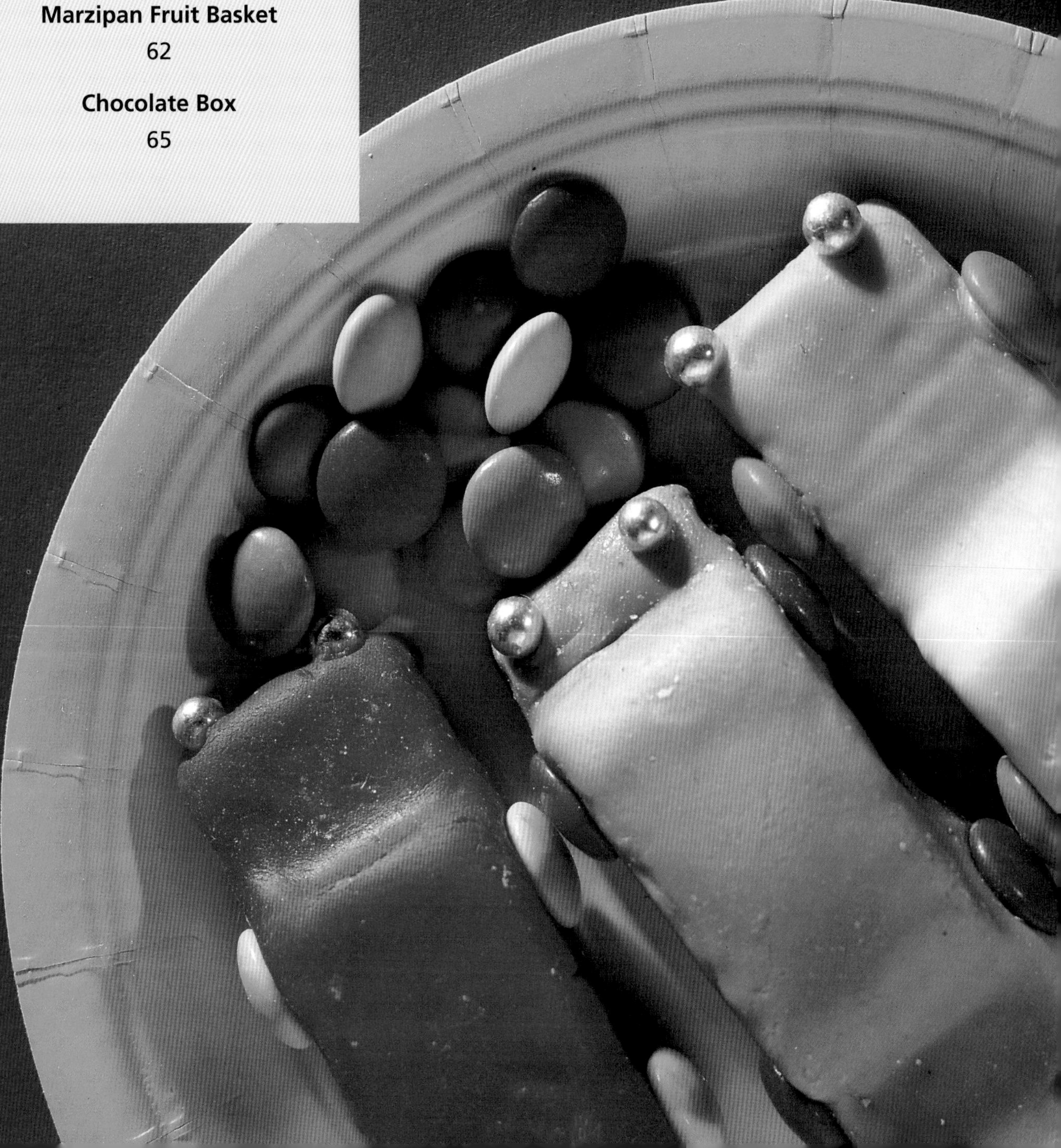

Cookie Car

It's fun to cook, but sometimes you want to make something quickly, perhaps to give to a special friend or for a party, when there is so much else to do. What could be more enjoyable than to make a car and then to eat it?

YOU WILL NEED

- Plain wafer cookies
- Blunt kitchen knife
- Jam (apricot or something similar)
- Spoon
- Ready-mixed icing sugar
- Food coloring: green
- Rolling pin
- 4 orange M & Ms®
- 4 silver balls (cake decorations)

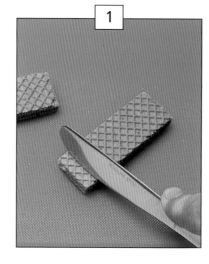

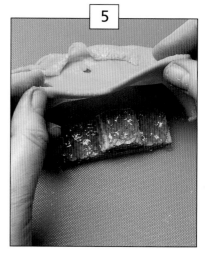

1 Take two wafer cookies and cut one of them in half. Trim the front and back of the short piece at an angle.

2 Place the cut piece of wafer on the whole piece and cover them both with jam.

3 Take a piece of ready-made icing sugar, about 1½ x 1½ inches, and mix in a little green food color, kneading it with your fingers until the color is evenly distributed through the icing.

4 Scatter a little icing sugar on the worktop and roll out the green icing sugar until it is large enough to cover the wafer biscuits.

5 Carefully lift the icing sugar over the biscuits.

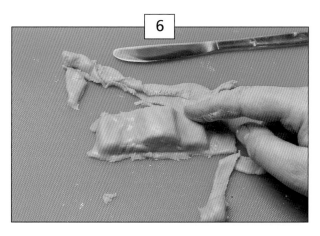

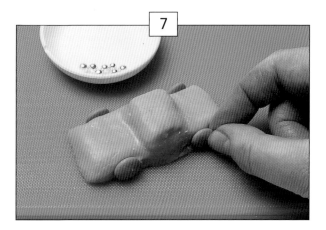

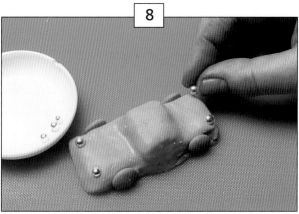

7 Use small pieces of softened icing sugar to attach orange M & Ms® to the bottom of the car to resemble wheels.

8 Place a silver ball in each corner to look like lights.

6 With your fingers, gently press the icing sugar onto the biscuits. Do not press too hard, but make the slopes clear. Trim around the edges with a knife.

Marzipan Fruit Basket

Working with marzipan is a little like working with modeling clay – except you can eat it. It is easy to use and can be bought ready made. You can color it with food coloring and then use it to make animals and flowers. Decorate it with small candies, nuts, and raisins to make them extra delicious.

YOU WILL NEED

- Block of white marzipan
- Kitchen knife
- Food coloring: green, red, orange, yellow, blue
- Teaspoon
- Toothpick
- Kitchen grater (optional)
- Paintbrushes
- Cloves
- Plastic box and netting
- Narrow ribbon

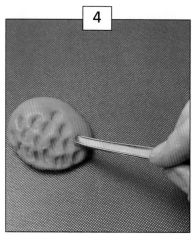

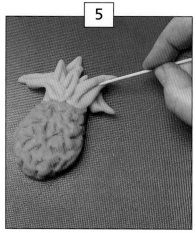

1 **Divide the block of marzipan into five equal pieces** and soften each piece by rolling it in your hands.

2 Flatten each piece and make a slight indentation in the center of each with your finger. Add some yellow coloring to one, some red to another, some green to another and some orange to another. Mix red and blue together to color the final piece purple.

3 Knead each color so that the color is distributed evenly through the marzipan.

4 Begin with orange marzipan and make the pineapple. Mold a piece into an egg shape and use the end of a teaspoon to make a pattern over the surface.

5 Roll some little tubes of green marzipan. Flatten one end and make a point at the other. Press the leaves to the top of the pineapple, arranging them to form a spray.

= 62 =

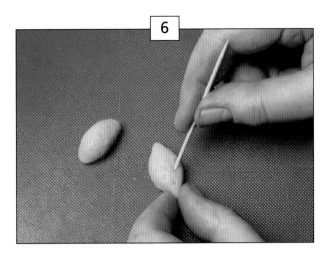

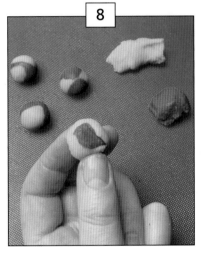

6 Use the yellow marzipan to make four or five bananas and about two lemons. Mold the lemons into little egg shapes with pointed ends, then make a pattern of tiny indentations all over the surface with the point of a toothpick. Or, press each one against the finest side of a kitchen grater.

7 Mold the remaining yellow into the shape of the bananas. Mix a tiny amount of brown coloring from the red, blue, and green, and use a fine brush to draw lines along the sides and to color in the ends.

8 Take small pieces of red and green and roll them together, taking care that the colors do not completely run together, to make apples. Make pears from the green marzipan, molding them with your fingers.

9 Make some balls of different sizes from the purple marzipan. These are going to be arranged into a bunch of grapes. Press the larger balls together to make a triangle. Put smaller balls on top to build up the bunch.

10 Use the red marzipan to make little strawberries. Make a pattern of indentations over the surface with a cocktail stick and attach little green leaves to the top.

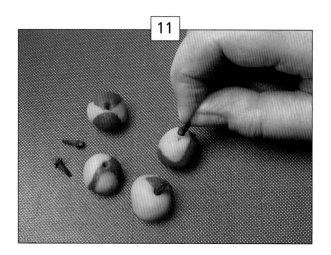

11 Use a toothpick to make an indentation in the top of the apples, grapes, pears, and bananas. Insert cloves in to the tops to represent stalks.

12 Place all the fruit in a small box or basket, arranging them so that the sides of the box are hidden. Tie a piece of netting over the box and hold it in place with a neat bow of narrow ribbon.

TIP

☞ Use any orange marzipan that is left to make oranges. Dimple the surface with a toothpick or grater in the same way as the lemons.

Chocolate Box

This is an ideal project to make for a present for a relative or friend. The chocolates are made in molds, and you can decorate the box in whatever way you want. You could put someone's name on it, or decorate it with shells, ribbons, or flowers. We used silver squares and sequins, which give a sophisticated look to the box, but you could use different colors or a different pattern.

YOU WILL NEED

- Large bar of chocolate (plain, milk, or nut)
- Heatproof bowl
- Saucepan
- Metal spoon
- Selection of chocolate molds
- Silver balls (cake decorations)
- Silver and purple foil
- Ruler
- Pencil
- Purple cardboard
- Cardboard box (empty chocolate box, for example)
- Scissors
- Craft glue and brush
- Silver cardboard
- Silver sequins
- Tissue paper
- Silver ribbon

1 Break the chocolate into pieces and place them in a heatproof bowl.

2 **Stand the bowl in a saucepan full of boiling water. Ask an adult to help you with this stage.**

3 When the chocolate is completely melted, spoon it into special chocolate molds. Place the molds in a freezer for about 1½ hours. If you put them in a refrigerator, it will take longer for the chocolate to set.

4 Remove the chocolate from the molds by tapping them sharply on your worktop.

5 Use a little melted chocolate to stick silver balls on the chocolate.

6 Wrap some of the chocolates in silver and purple foil.

7 Use a ruler to mark pieces of purple cardboard that will exactly cover the sides and top of the box.

8 Cut out the pieces of cardboard. Remember to include a piece that will cover the inside of the lid.

9 Glue the purple cardboard over the top and sides of the box.

10 Use a ruler to make a grid of squares, about ¾ x ¾ inch, on the silver cardboard. You will need about 52 squares. Cut out the squares, making sure that the edges are neat and straight.

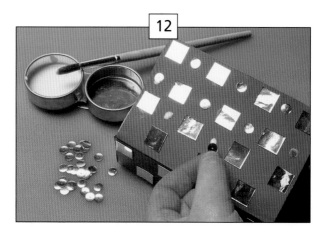

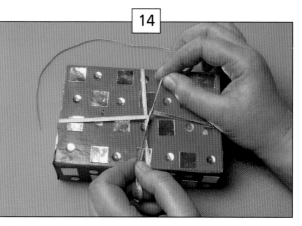

11 Stick the squares in rows on the top and sides of the box.

12 Stick a sequin between each silver square.

13 Put some tissue paper in the bottom of the box and place a layer of chocolates in the box. Cover the chocolates with a piece of silver cardboard and add a second layer of chocolates.

14 Tie a length of silver ribbon around the box and tie a neat bow.

Rainforest Scene

When you go for a walk in the countryside or along the seashore, you will find all kinds of interesting things – feathers, shells, pebbles, stones, cones, the list is almost endless. You may not have all the items we have used for our rainforest, but our layout will give you ideas for your own version. Let the materials you have suggest ways in which you can develop your own model.

YOU WILL NEED

- Corks
- Craft knife
- Craft glue
- Twigs
- Feathers
- Fine cord
- Black felt-tipped pen
- Pine cones
- Screw-in eyes
- Shallow tray or box
- Blue or green construction paper
- Sand (optional)
- Plasticine
- Grasses, leaves, etc.
- Shells, pebbles, small stones, etc.
- Pieces of bark or driftwood
- Scraps of fabric: red and white
- Scissors

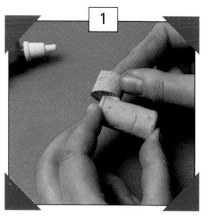

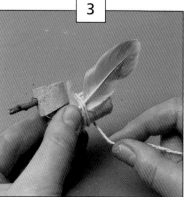

1 **Cut one of the corks in half. If you use a craft knife, ask an adult to help.** Stick the half cork onto a whole cork to form the body and head of a bird.

2 Use a twig to make a hole for the beak in the smaller of the corks. Break the twig until it is about ¾ inch long and glue it in the hole.

3 Bind a feather to the side of the bird's body with fine cord. Mark the bird's eyes on the small cork with a pen.

4 Remove some of the scales from a large pine cone.

5 Stick a scale on each side of another cork. Use a piece of twig to make a beak (see step 3) and stick a feather on top of the cork.

6 Draw in eyes with a felt-tipped pen. Insert a screw eye at the back of the cork so that you can hang the bird up.

7 Make the base of the picture in a shallow tray or box with a rim about ¾ inch deep. Cover the base with blue or green paper, or use a different color at each end

and disguise the join by applying a thin layer of glue down the center and shaking sand over it. Shake off any excess sand.

8 Use pieces of Plasticine to make bases for the dried grasses and leaves. Arrange them at the back of the box.

9 Arrange the pebbles, shells, and so on in front of the vegetation. Hang the birds in the trees.

10 Stick a twig in the middle of a piece of bark or small piece of driftwood.

11 Bind cord around the base of the boat and the twig to hold the twig firm.

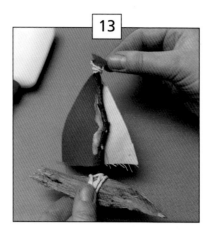

12 Run a line of glue along the twig. Stick the sails in place on the twig.

13 Bind the top of the sails with a piece of fine cord. Cut out and glue in place a tiny flag or pennant for the top of the mast.

14 Place the boat at the front of the arrangement. Try making a raft from twigs and scrap fabric. Add some shells and bits of coral to the ocean end of your model.

Great Greeting Card

Sometimes you want to make something quickly, and this card is ideal. It makes use of the odds and ends you might have collected, such as dried flowers or brightly colored feathers. Choose different colored papers for the base to create a quite different effect.

YOU WILL NEED

- Colored cardboard: yellow and orange
- White cardboard
- Scissors
- Craft glue
- Dried flowers
- Feathers
- Shells

1 Cut a large rectangle of yellow cardboard for the background and fold it carefully in two.

2 Copy the template from page 93 and transfer the outline to stiff cardboard.

3 Cut around the shape in orange cardboard, making sure that the edges are smooth.

4 Stick the orange cardboard to the center of the front of the yellow cardboard.

5 Glue dried flowers to the orange cardboard.

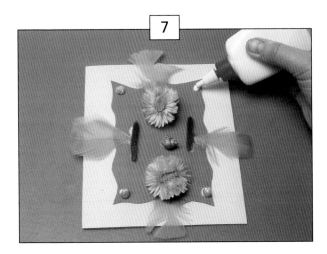

8 Glue on some little shells. Make sure that the glue is dry before moving the cardboard or writing your message inside.

6 Add feathers and shells in a pattern. It is a good idea to try out several arrangements before gluing anything down. Glue on the feathers.

7 Put a dab of glue at each corner.

Cork Necklace

Cork is an excellent material for making jewelry, mainly because it is so easy to make holes in it. It is light and soft, and you do not need complicated tools to work with it. You can leave the cork as it is, or combine it with all kinds of beads and feathers.

YOU WILL NEED

- Craft knife
- 4–5 corks
- Knitting needle
- Paints: white, blue, black, silver, turquoise
- Paintbrushes
- Fine wire (fuse wire)
- Feathers and beads
- Narrow elastic

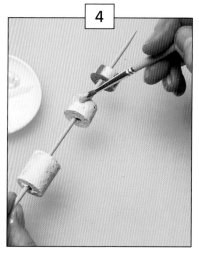

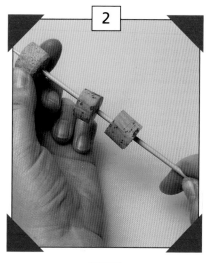

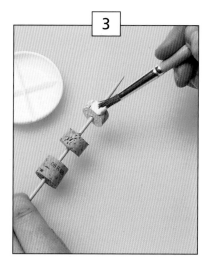

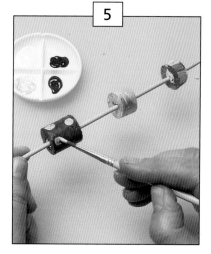

1 **Use a craft knife to cut the corks into various sizes.** The necklace will look more interesting if they are not all the same size. Ask an adult to help you with this.

2 **Thread the corks onto a knitting needle** so that it is easier to paint them. **Take**

care not to push the point of the knitting needle against your hand.

3 Give each cork a coat of white paint and leave to dry. This will make the finished color stronger, although you can skip this stage if you want.

4 Paint some of the corks dark blue (blue and black), some silver, and some turquoise. Leave to dry.

5 Decorate the "beads" with spots and stripes of different colors. Try mixing blue paint with silver to create some interesting effects.

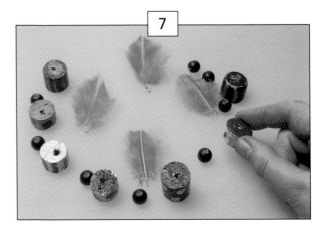

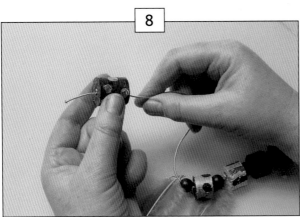

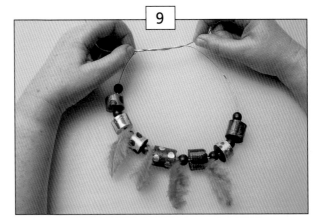

6 Use short lengths of fine metal wire to make loops through the feathers.

7 Arrange the beads, feathers, and pieces of cork as you would like them to be. Make sure that the arrangement will be long enough to go around your neck.

8 When you are satisfied with the arrangement, begin to thread the beads, cork, and feathers onto the elastic. The holes in the cork made by the knitting needle will be large enough for you to thread the elastic through.

9 Tie the ends of the elastic together in a neat bow.

CHAPTER SEVEN

Balsa Wood

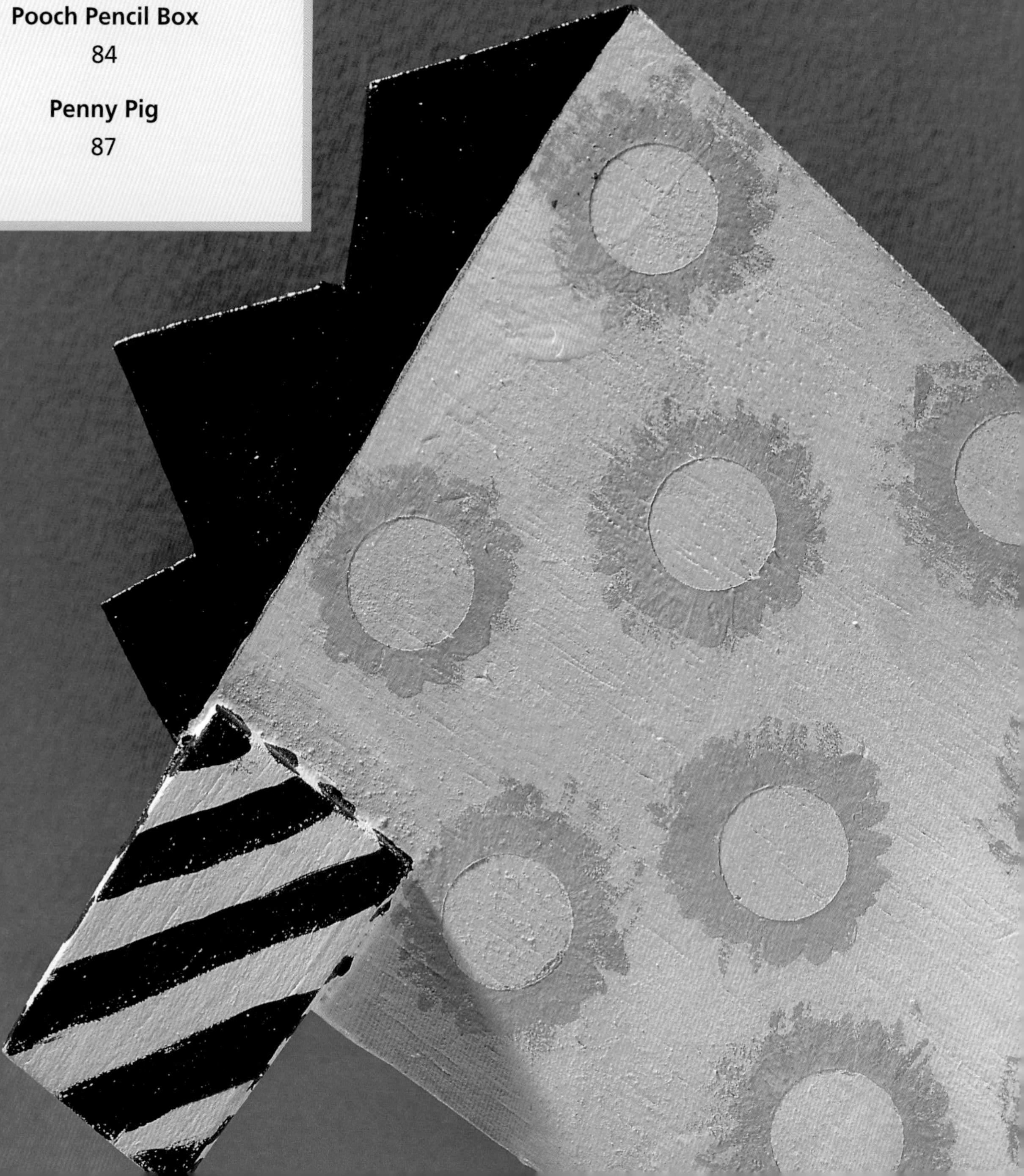

Fly Away!

This glider is a simple project to start off with. It's only got three basic pieces, but it has been designed so that it will fly really well. If you find that you cannot get it to fly smoothly, try adding different weights – paper clips or small pieces of Plasticine, for example – on each side of the nose.

YOU WILL NEED

- Pencil
- White cardboard
- Scissors
- Balsa wood: 1 thin sheet (⅛ inch)
- Craft knife
- Sandpaper
- Plasticine
- Paints: white, blue, black
- Paintbrushes
- Adhesive paper, stars, and circles
- Varnish and brush

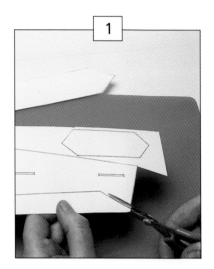

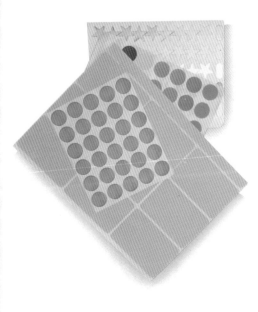

1 Copy the templates on page 94 and transfer the outlines to cardboard. Cut out the pieces.

2 Draw around the cardboard templates to transfer the outlines of the pieces to the balsa wood. Remember to include the slits that have to be cut.

3 **Use a craft knife and ruler to cut out all the pieces.** Use four or five gentle cuts rather than one strong one.

4 **Carefully cut out the slits in the plane's body.**

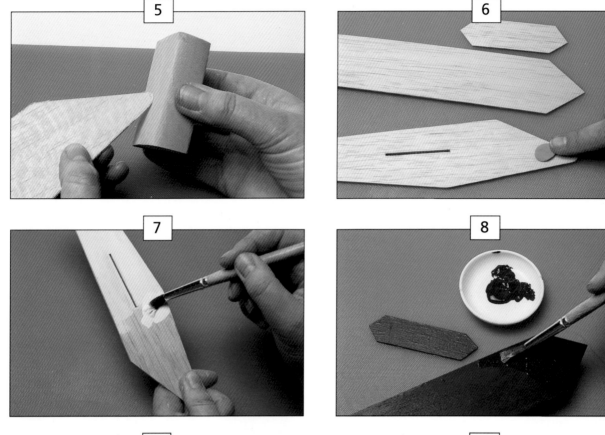

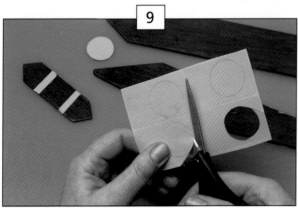

5 Smooth any rough edges with fine sandpaper to give a more aerodynamic shape. Work carefully because the wood is very thin.

6 Place a small piece of Plasticine on each side of the nose as marked on the template. The extra weight will help the glider to fly well.

7 Paint all the pieces with white paint on both sides. Leave to dry.

8 Mix some dark blue paint (blue and black) to paint all three pieces. Leave the paint to dry.

9 Cut some shapes from adhesive paper if you cannot find ready-made ones in the size or color you want.

10 Finish the decoration by adding self-adhesive stars, circles, and so on.

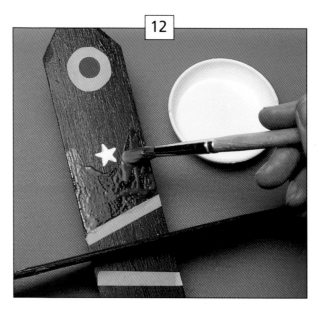

11 Assemble the pieces, sliding the wings through the hole in the fuselage and the tail in the tail piece.

12 Finish by applying at least one coat of varnish to seal the decoration. Remember to allow the first coat of varnish to dry before you apply the next. When the varnish is dry, give your glider a trial flight.

Letter Rack

This is an excellent project for developing your woodworking skills. The simple design is easy to make once you have got used to cutting out the shapes. The paint design was inspired by the design on airmail paper.

YOU WILL NEED

- Ruler
- Pencil
- Balsa wood: 1 sheet each medium (¼ inch) and thin (⅛ inch)
- Craft knife
- Balsa wood adhesive
- Pins
- Sandpaper
- Small block of wood
- Thumbtack
- Paints: white, blue, red
- Paintbrushes
- Varnish and brush

Runner – cut 4   ¼ inch

8¼ inches

Back – cut 1   4 inches

¾ inch

1 inch

Decorative square – cut 7

Base – cut 1   3 inches

Front – cut 1   2½ inches

NOT TO SCALE

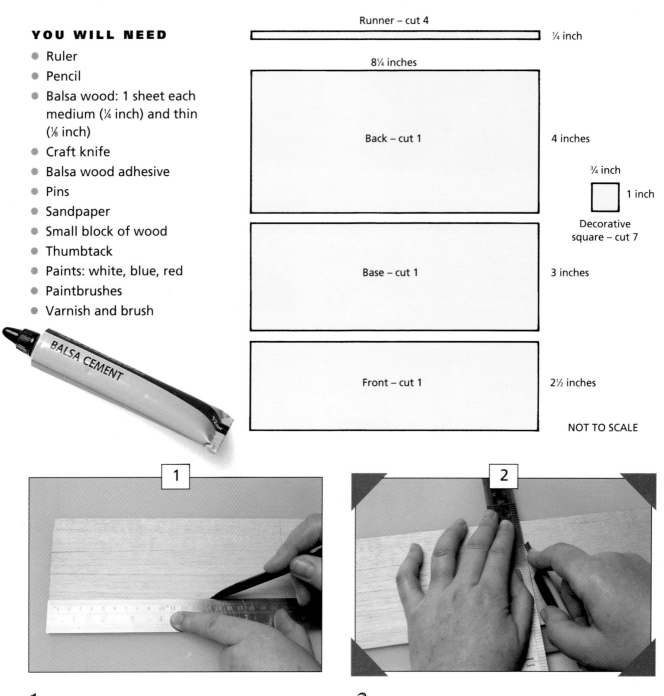

1 Measure out the front, back, and base sections on medium balsa wood, following the cutting diagram, above.

2 Use a craft knife to cut out the pieces. Make several small cuts rather than one strong cut. Press down against the ruler.

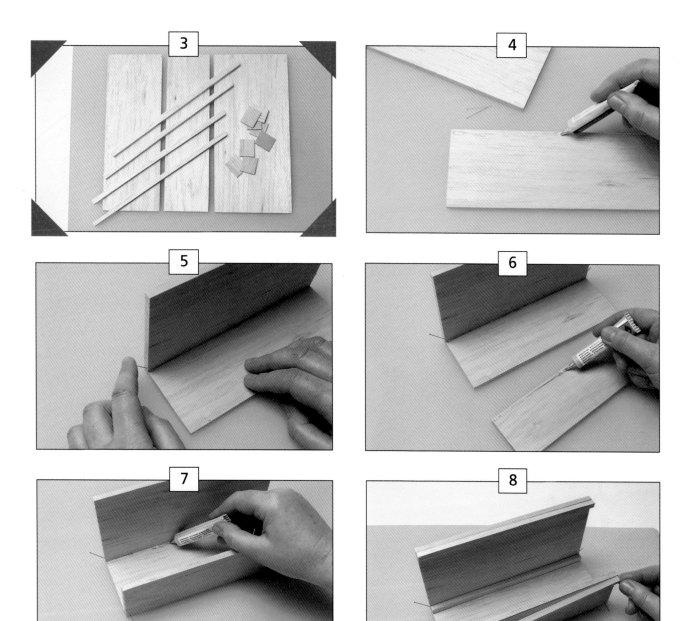

3 **Cut four sticks from the medium wood and seven small squares from the thin wood.** Lay all the pieces out to make sure you have everything you need.

4 Glue the back to the base. Use quite a lot of glue to hold the joints together.

5 Use pins to hold the pieces together. Make sure that the pieces are at right angles.

6 Glue and pin the front to the base in the same way.

7 When the main pieces are dry, which should not take long, glue two of the long, thin pieces along the inside of the joins to strengthen the letter rack.

8 Glue and pin the other two strips along the tops of the front and back. Leave to dry and then remove all the pins.

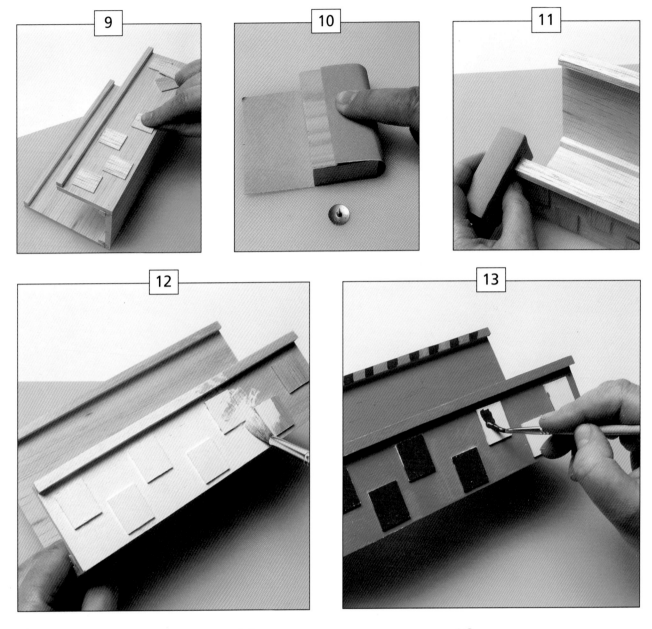

9 Glue the squares over the front of the letter rack, making sure they are evenly spaced. Do not use too much glue, or it will ooze out when you press them down.

10 Make a sanding block by wrapping a piece of sandpaper around a small block of wood and securing it with a thumbtack.

11 Gently sand all the edges and surfaces to give a smooth finish.

12 Apply a coat of white paint to all surfaces. Paint the background light blue (blue and white).

13 Paint the squares red and add some red stripes along the fronts of the two thin wooden strips.

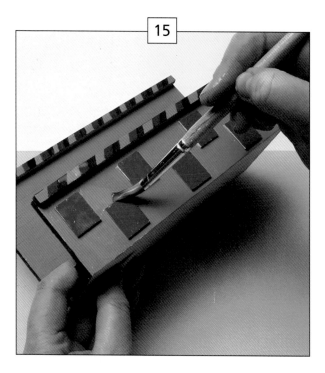

14 Mix dark blue (blue and black) and paint the top surfaces of the two thin strips and the sides of the letter rack. Add dark blue stripes next to the red stripes.

15 When the paint is dry, varnish all over.

Pooch Pencil Box

If you feel pretty confident making models from balsa wood, then why not have a try at this delightful doggy box? Because you need thicker wood to model the head, you will need a junior hacksaw to cut the wood – take care, as always, with sharp tools.

YOU WILL NEED

- White cardboard
- Scissors
- Pencil
- Balsa wood: 1 sheet each thick (½ inch), medium (¼ inch), and thin (⅛ inch)
- Junior hacksaw
- Ruler
- Craft knife
- Balsa wood adhesive
- Pins
- Sandpaper
- Paints: white, red, black
- Paintbrushes
- Varnish and brush

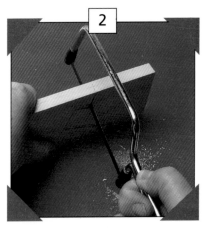

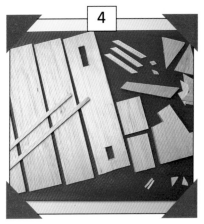

1 Copy the templates of the dog's head and features on page 95 and transfer them to thick cardboard. Cut out all the pieces. Draw around the outline of the template of the dog's head onto the piece of thick balsa wood.

2 **Use a hacksaw to cut around the outline. Ask an adult to help with this because the wood is quite thick.**

3 Measure out the sides, lid, ends, base, and runners on medium balsa wood, using the cutting diagram as a guide. **Cut the pieces out with a craft knife.**

4 **Use the other cardboard templates to cut out all the decorative pieces** – nose, eyes, ears, and collar – from the thin balsa wood. Lay out all the pieces you have cut to check that everything is there.

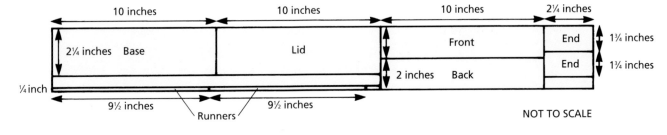

10 inches	10 inches	10 inches	2¼ inches

2¼ inches Base   Lid   Front / Back   End / End

1¾ inches / 1¾ inches

2 inches Back

¼ inch

9½ inches   Runners   9½ inches

NOT TO SCALE

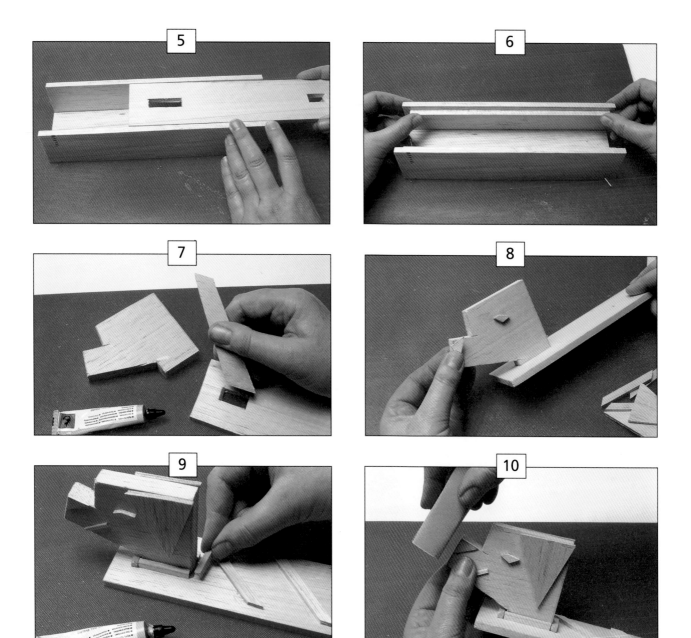

5 Glue then pin the sides to the base. Check that the lid fits between the sides.

6 Measure down about ¼ inch from the top edge of the box. Draw a line at this depth to mark the position of the top of the runners. Glue and pin the runners in place before gluing and pinning the ends on.

7 Glue the dog's tail in position on the box lid. It should be about ¾ inch from one end.

8 Glue the dog's head at the other end, making sure it is the same distance from the end as the tail.

9 Glue the three strips across the top of the box, angling

them slightly. Glue them in place. Arrange the other decorative pieces on the dog's head and on the box and then glue them in place.

10 When the glue is dry, carefully sand the surface of the dog and box. It is sometimes easier to smooth the surfaces of the small pieces before they are glued in place.

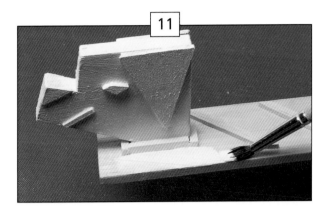

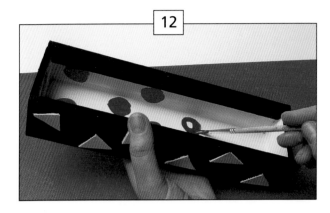

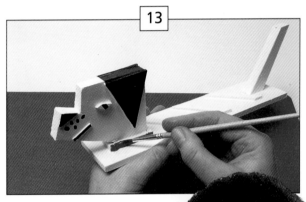

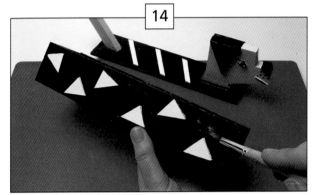

11 Paint the box white, inside and out.

12 Leaving the triangles white, paint the base of the box black. Paint some red circles inside.

13 Paint the dog's features black and add some dots around the nose to represent whiskers. Paint the collar red, then paint the top of the box black, leaving the three stripes white.

14 When the paint is dry, varnish all over, inside and out.

Penny Pig

This is the most difficult of the balsa wood projects, but it does make a great working piggy bank. We have made it as easy to get your money out as it is to put it in. There is a simple sliding door mechanism at one end, running between two sets of runners, in the same way that a drawer runs in and out.

YOU WILL NEED

- White cardboard
- Scissors
- Pencil
- Balsa wood: 1 sheet each medium (¼ inch) and thin (⅛ inch)
- Craft knife
- Balsa wood adhesive
- Pins
- Paints: white, red, black
- Paintbrushes
- White circular stickers
- Varnish and brush

4¼ inches

| Base – cut 1 | 1¼ inches |

4 inches

| Top – cut 1 | 1¼ inches |

2½ inches

| End – cut 2 |

Runner – cut 4
1¼ inches

¼ inch   NOT TO SCALE

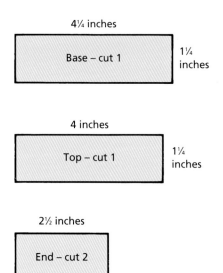

1 Copy the templates on page 96 and transfer the outlines to stiff cardboard. Cut out the templates.

2 Use the templates to draw around the outlines onto the balsa wood. Use the medium wood for the main construction – the pig-shaped sides – and the thin wood for details such as the eyes and ears.

3 **Cut out all the shapes with a craft knife. Go over each cut lightly several times rather than trying to cut through all at once. Cut a slit in the top of the box that is about ¼ inch wide and 1½ inch long.**

4 Finish cutting out all the pieces and lay them out to make sure you have everything, including ears, eyes, and legs.

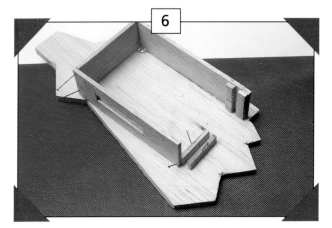

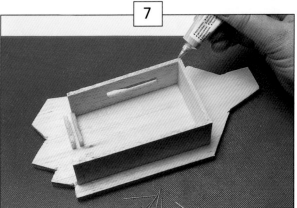

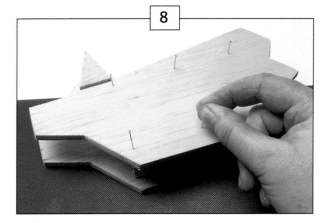

5 Glue the inner box base and end to one side of the pig. **Cut two small strips from the thin balsa wood** and glue them to the base of the box so that they are about ¼ inch apart. Check that the end piece slides easily between these two pieces.

6 **Cut two more strips, slightly longer,** and position them on the side of the box so that they align exactly with the two shorter strips. Glue and pin the top of the box in position. Glue and pin the runner in place. Check again that the end piece will slide easily between them and slot into the strips on the base.

7 Apply glue all the way round the edge of the box.

8 Place the other side of the pig in place. Glue on the ears and pin everything in position.

9 Glue on the eyes and legs, holding them in place with pins until the glue has dried.

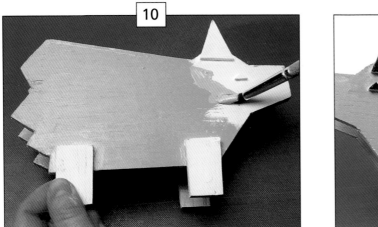

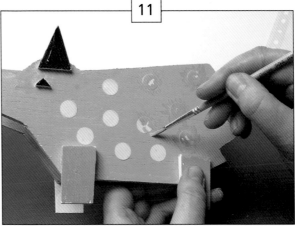

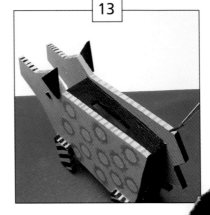

10 Paint the pig white all over. When the undercoat is dry, mix some pink paint (red and white) and paint the pig all over. Leave to dry. Paint the legs grey and the ears and eyes black. Put some white peel-off stickers on the pig's body when the pink paint is completely dry.

11 Carefully paint around the circles with grey, brushing the paint upwards to make a sort of halo effect. When the grey paint is dry, peel off the stickers.

12 Paint the pig's tail black. Paint fine, black, slanting stripes on the pig's legs.

13 Paint the box black, including the end piece which slides up and down, and decorate the top edge with black stripes.

14 When the paint is dry, varnish the piggy bank all over.

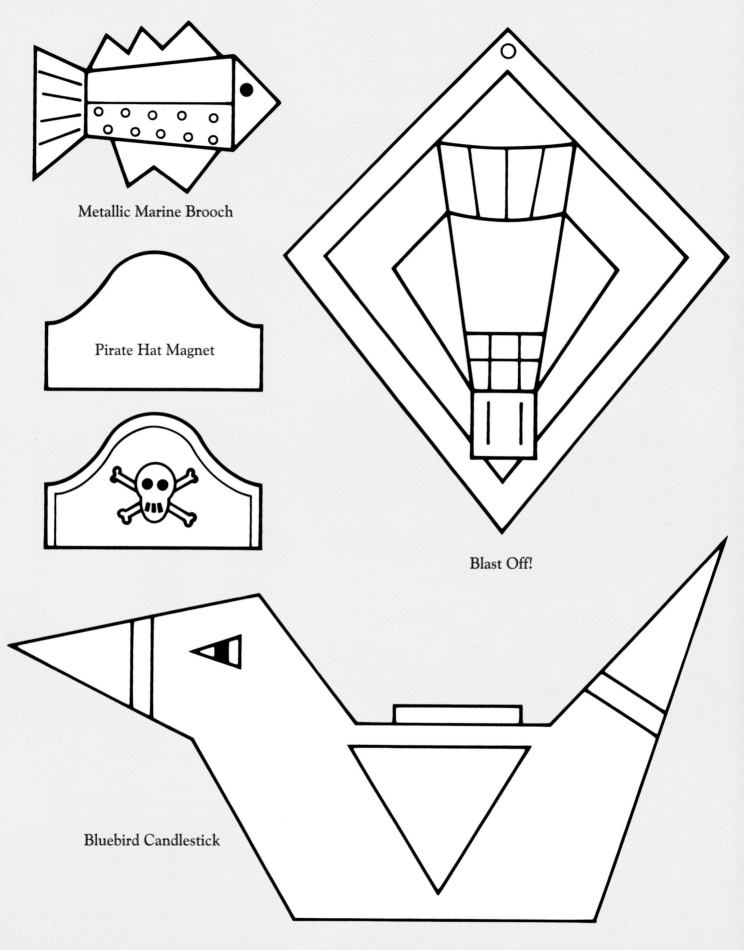

Metallic Marine Brooch

Pirate Hat Magnet

Blast Off!

Bluebird Candlestick

Dinosaur for
top of mobile

Score and bend.
Glue on to top of mobile

Dinosaur Mobile

Dinosaur Mobile

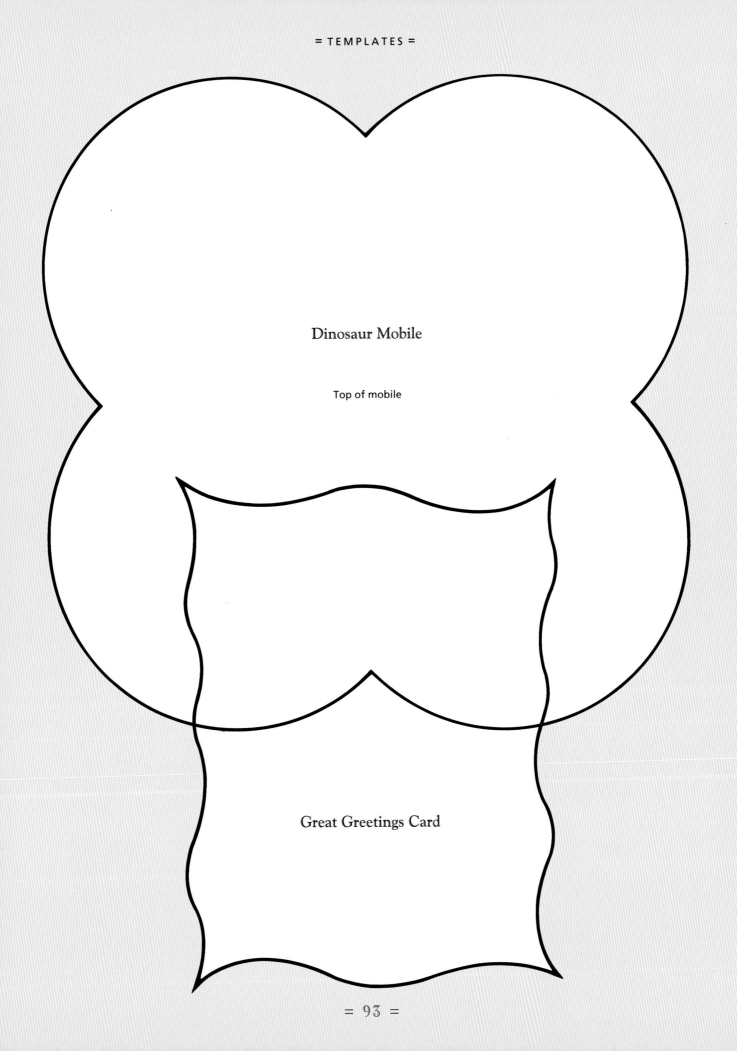

Dinosaur Mobile

Top of mobile

Great Greetings Card

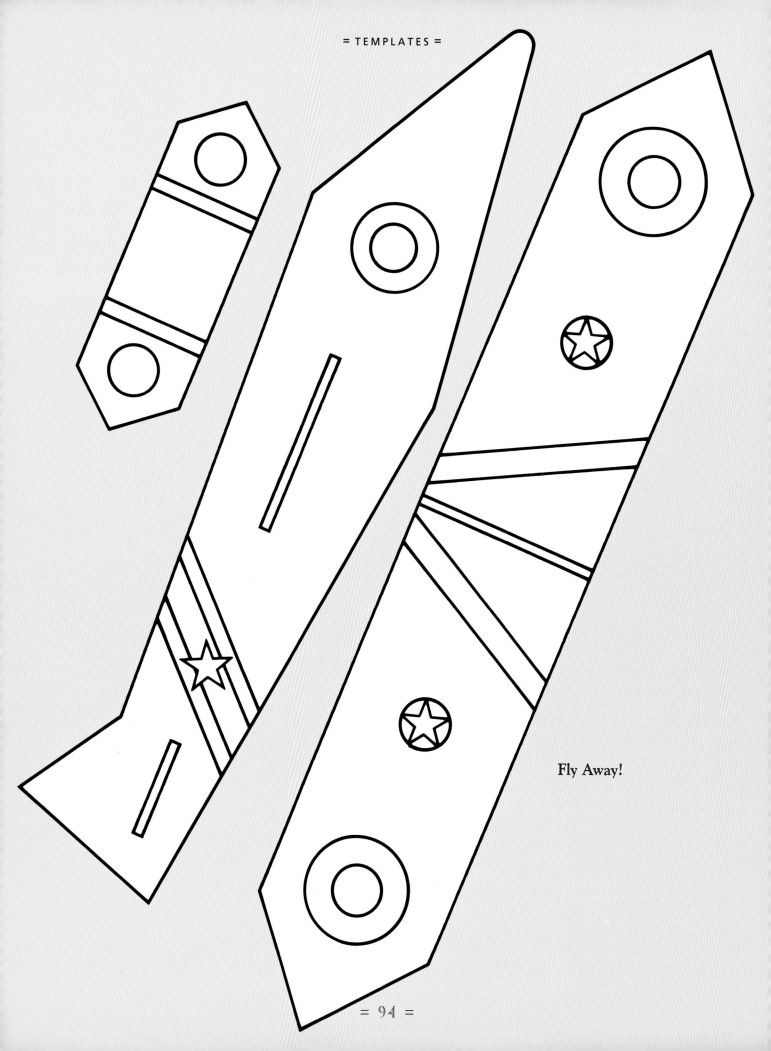

Fly Away!

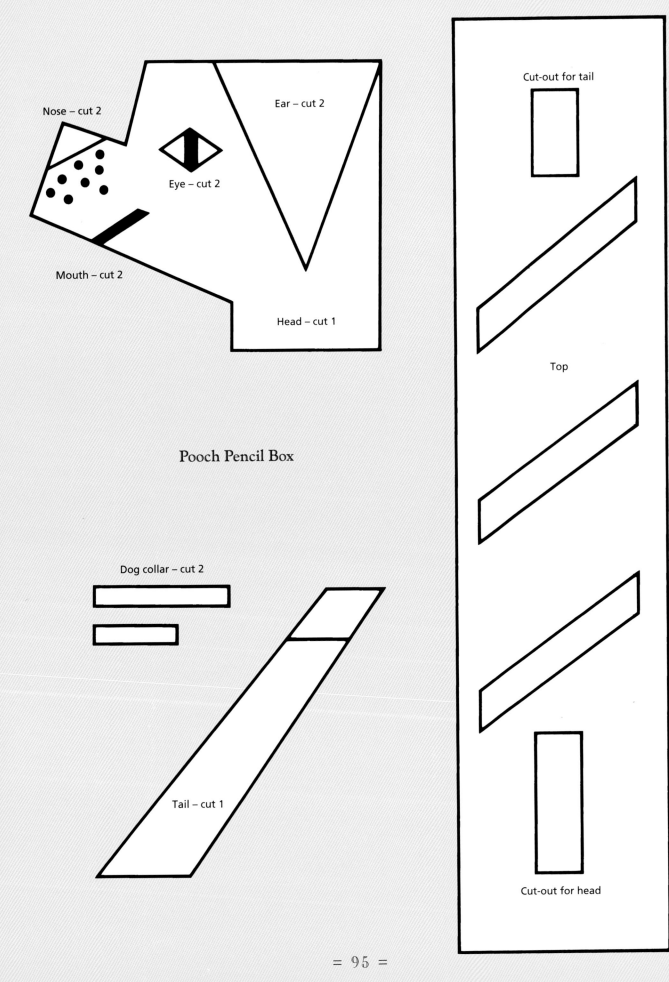

Nose – cut 2

Ear – cut 2

Eye – cut 2

Mouth – cut 2

Head – cut 1

Pooch Pencil Box

Dog collar – cut 2

Tail – cut 1

Cut-out for tail

Top

Cut-out for head

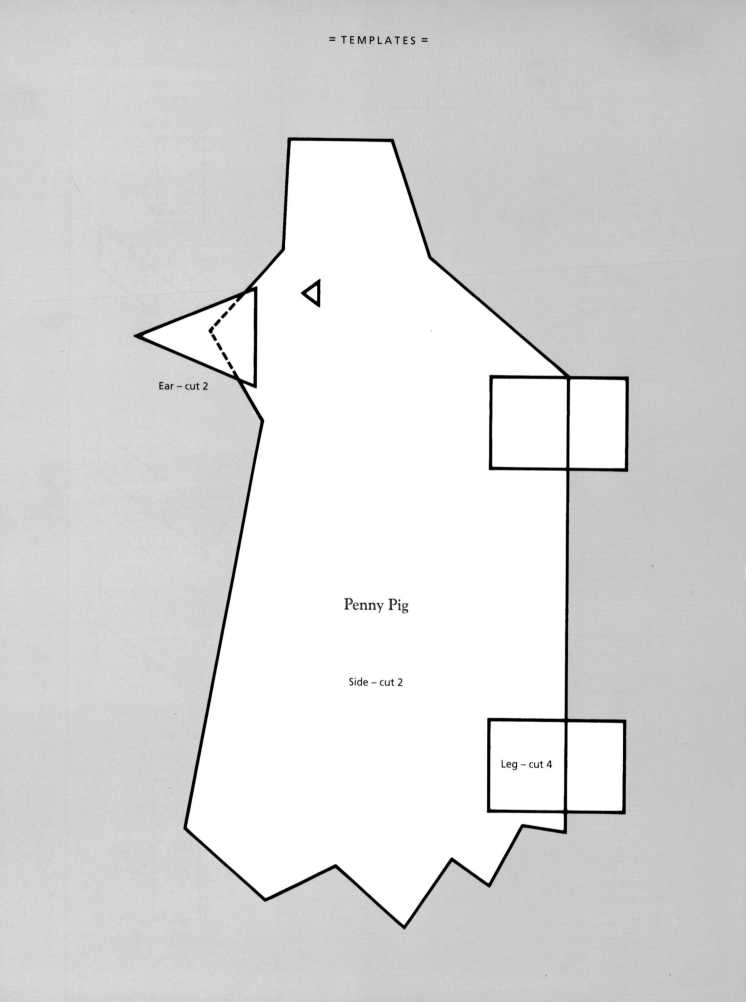

Ear – cut 2

Penny Pig

Side – cut 2

Leg – cut 4